MADRID TRAVEL GUIDE 2025

Exploring Iconic Landmarks, Local Flavors, and Unforgettable Experiences

Alec D. Shaw

Copyright © 2024 , Alec D. Shaw.

All rights reserved. No part of this publication may be reproduced, distributed, or transmitted in any form or by any means, including photocopying, recording, or other electronic or mechanical methods, without the prior written permission of the publisher, except in the case of brief quotations embodied in critical reviews and certain other non-commercial uses permitted by copyright law.

DISCLAIMER

The information in this book is for general guidance only. While every effort has been made to ensure accuracy at the time of publication, prices, schedules, and details may change. The author and publisher are not responsible for any errors, omissions, or changes that may occur, nor for any inconvenience or loss arising from the use of this guide. Readers are encouraged to verify details with relevant providers. Any external links or recommendations are for reference and do not constitute an endorsement.

TABLE OF CONTENT

Chapter 1: Introduction To Madrid
- Overview and Quick Facts
- Why Visit Madrid in 2025?
- Planning Essentials: When to Visit, Getting There, and Practical Tips

Chapter 2: Top Attractions And Cultural Highlights
- Historical Sites and Landmarks
- Museums and Art Galleries
- Parks and Gardens
- Cultural Experiences: Flamenco, Festivals, and Performing Arts

Chapter 3: Where To Stay And Getting Around
- Best Neighborhoods to Stay
- Accommodation Options in Madrid
- Hotel Recommendation Across Madrid
- Public Transportation and Getting Around Madrid

Chapter 4: Madrid For Foodies And Shoppers
- Must-Try Dishes and Top Restaurants
- Food Markets and Street Food

- ❖ Shopping Districts and Souvenirs

Chapter 5: Day Trips And Hidden Gems
- ❖ Best Day Trips: Toledo, Segovia, El Escorial, and More
- ❖ Off the Beaten Path: Hidden Neighborhoods and Unique Experiences
- ❖ Family-Friendly Activities and Attractions

Chapter 6: Practical Information And Resources
- ❖ Health, Safety, and Accessibility
- ❖ Budgeting Tips and Free Things to Do
- ❖ Maps, Suggested Itineraries, and Useful Apps

CHAPTER ONE
INTRODUCTION TO MADRID

Overview and Quick Facts

Madrid, the bustling capital of Spain, is a city where history and modernity coexist in perfect harmony. With its rich cultural heritage, vibrant nightlife, and world-renowned art scene, Madrid is a destination that offers something for everyone. The city, home to approximately 3.3 million people, expands to over 6.6 million in its metropolitan area, making it one of the largest and most dynamic cities in Europe.

The official language spoken in Madrid is Spanish (Castilian), and the currency used is the Euro (€). Visitors will find that the city's Mediterranean climate is characterized by hot summers and mild winters. Summer temperatures often soar to around 30°C (86°F), while winters are more temperate, with averages hovering around 10°C (50°F). This pleasant weather, coupled with the city's extensive public transportation system—including a well-connected metro, buses, and taxis—makes Madrid a comfortable and accessible destination for tourists.

Madrid is a city steeped in history, with landmarks such as the Royal Palace, the Prado Museum, and Plaza Mayor serving as testaments to its illustrious past. The iconic Gran Via, with its impressive architecture and bustling atmosphere, exemplifies Madrid's blend of the old and the new. Visitors can stroll through Retiro Park, one of the city's most beloved green spaces, or immerse themselves in the artistic treasures found within the Golden Triangle of Art, which includes the Prado, Reina Sofia, and Thyssen-Bornemisza Museums.

Culinary delights are another highlight of Madrid. The city's gastronomy is a reflection of its rich cultural tapestry, offering everything from traditional tapas to more refined dishes like Cocido Madrileño, a hearty chickpea-based stew, and Churros con Chocolate, a beloved treat. Jamón Ibérico, one of Spain's most prized delicacies, is also a must-try for any food lover. With a dining scene that spans from casual tapas bars to Michelin-starred restaurants, Madrid is a paradise for food enthusiasts.

Safety in Madrid is generally good, with the city being considered one of the safer European capitals. However, like any major urban area, visitors should be mindful of pickpockets, particularly in crowded tourist spots. The city is known for its vibrant nightlife, earning its reputation as a place that never sleeps. From traditional taverns to contemporary rooftop bars, Madrid offers a diverse array of venues where visitors can experience its lively nocturnal culture.

The year 2025 promises to be an especially exciting time to visit Madrid. The city continues to be a hub for cultural events, with annual highlights such as the San Isidro Festival and Madrid Pride drawing visitors from around the world. Additionally, new attractions and developments are expected to further enhance the city's appeal. Expanded museum exhibits, modern public spaces, and innovative architectural projects will ensure that Madrid remains at the forefront of global cultural destinations.

Madrid is a city that captivates with its rich history, dynamic culture, and inviting atmosphere. Whether you are drawn to its art and architecture, its culinary offerings, or simply the vibrant energy that pulses through its streets, Madrid is a city that promises to leave a lasting impression on every traveler.

Why Visit Madrid in 2025?

Madrid, the heart of Spain, has long been a magnet for travelers seeking a blend of history, culture, and modern vibrancy. As the city continues to evolve, 2025 presents an especially compelling time to visit. With new developments, cultural events, and an ever-growing culinary scene, Madrid promises an experience that is both timeless and fresh.

One of the most enticing reasons to visit Madrid in 2025 is the array of cultural events that will take place throughout the year. Madrid is a city that thrives on celebration, and its calendar is packed with festivals that showcase its rich heritage and contemporary spirit. The San Isidro Festival, held every May, is a quintessential Madrid experience. It's a time when the city honors its patron saint with parades, music, and traditional dances, offering visitors a chance to immerse themselves in authentic Spanish culture. Additionally, Madrid Pride, one of the largest LGBTQ+ celebrations in Europe, transforms the city into a vibrant and inclusive party, attracting hundreds of thousands of people from around the world.

2025 will also see the unveiling of new attractions and significant upgrades to existing ones, making it an ideal year for both first-time visitors and returning travelers. The city's renowned museums, such as the Prado and Reina Sofia, are expected to introduce expanded exhibits and special collections, further cementing Madrid's status as a global arts capital. New public spaces and architectural projects will also be completed, reflecting Madrid's commitment to blending tradition with innovation. These developments will offer fresh perspectives on the city's cultural landscape, providing new opportunities for exploration and discovery.

Madrid's culinary scene continues to flourish, making it a paradise for food enthusiasts. In 2025, the city will likely see the opening of new restaurants and the continued rise of Madrid's position as a gastronomic hub. Whether you're sampling tapas in a traditional tavern or indulging in avant-garde dishes at a Michelin-starred restaurant, Madrid's food scene offers an experience that is both diverse and deeply rooted in Spanish tradition. The city's food markets, such as Mercado de San Miguel and Mercado de San Antón, will continue to be popular spots where visitors can taste the flavors of Spain in a lively, communal setting.

Moreover, Madrid's nightlife, famous for its energy and variety, will continue to draw night owls and party-goers. The city is known for its late nights, with bars, clubs, and live music venues buzzing until the early hours. In 2025, the nightlife scene is expected to be as vibrant as ever, with new venues and rooftop bars offering stunning views of the city skyline. Madrid's reputation as a city that never sleeps will be alive and well, providing endless options for those looking to experience the city after dark.

In terms of accessibility, Madrid remains one of Europe's most well-connected cities. Its efficient public transportation system makes it easy to explore both the city center and the surrounding areas. Whether you're interested in taking a day trip to the historic towns of Toledo or Segovia or exploring the modern developments within the city itself, getting around Madrid is convenient and straightforward.

Finally, 2025 will be a year when Madrid's role on the global stage is highlighted through international events and conferences. As a city that regularly hosts major exhibitions, business meetings, and cultural forums, Madrid will continue to be a key player in global discourse. For travelers interested in being at the center of world events, 2025 is an opportune time to experience Madrid's dynamic and international atmosphere.

In summary, 2025 is set to be an extraordinary year for visiting Madrid. With its vibrant cultural calendar, new attractions, thriving culinary scene, and enduring charm, Madrid offers a travel experience that is both enriching and unforgettable. Whether you're drawn by its history, its modernity, or simply the energy that permeates its streets, Madrid in 2025 promises to be a destination that captivates and inspires.

Planning Essentials

When to Visit Madrid

Madrid is a city that offers something special throughout the year, but the best time to visit depends on your preferences for weather, events, and crowd levels.

Spring (March to May): Spring is arguably the best time to visit Madrid. The weather is mild, with temperatures ranging from 12°C to 21°C (54°F to 70°F). The city's parks, such as El Retiro, are in full bloom, and outdoor cafes and terraces are bustling. Spring also marks the beginning of the festival season, with events like the San Isidro Festival in May, celebrating the city's patron saint with parades, concerts, and traditional activities.

Summer (June to August): Summer in Madrid can be hot, with temperatures often exceeding 30°C (86°F). Despite the heat, this is a popular time for tourists, especially in July and August when many locals leave the city for holidays. Summer brings a lively atmosphere with numerous outdoor events, including concerts, open-air cinema, and street festivals. However, some smaller shops and restaurants may close during August.

Autumn (September to November): Fall is another excellent time to visit Madrid, with cooler temperatures between 10°C and 20°C (50°F to 68°F) and fewer tourists. The city is particularly beautiful as the leaves change color in its many parks. Cultural events continue in full swing, and this is a great time for food lovers to enjoy seasonal Spanish dishes.

Winter (December to February): Winters in Madrid are mild, with temperatures ranging from 5°C to 12°C (41°F to 54°F). While it's not as warm as in other seasons, Madrid's Christmas markets, festive lights, and New Year celebrations make it a magical time to visit. Additionally, winter is the off-peak tourist season, so you'll find fewer crowds and better deals on accommodation.

Getting There

Madrid is one of Europe's most accessible cities, with numerous transportation options to get you there.

By Air: Madrid-Barajas Adolfo Suárez Airport (MAD) is the main international gateway to the city, located about 12 kilometers (7.5 miles) northeast of the city center. It is one of the busiest airports in Europe, serving flights from all over the world. The airport is well-connected to the city center by metro, train, and bus services, making it easy to reach your accommodation upon arrival.

By Train: Madrid is a major hub in Spain's high-speed train network, known as AVE (Alta Velocidad Española). You can travel to Madrid from major cities like Barcelona, Seville, and Valencia in just a few hours. The main train station, Atocha, is located in the heart of the city and is a key point for both national and international rail services.

By Bus: Long-distance buses connect Madrid with many European cities, as well as towns and cities across Spain. The main bus stations, Estación Sur and Méndez Álvaro, are well-connected to the metro system, making it easy to reach your final destination within the city.

By Car: If you prefer to drive, Madrid is accessible by a network of highways. However, driving in the city can be challenging due to traffic and limited parking, so it's generally recommended to use public transportation once you arrive.

CHAPTER TWO
Top Attractions And Cultural Highlights
Historical Sites and Landmarks in Madrid

Madrid, a city with a rich tapestry of history, is home to numerous historical sites and landmarks that tell the story of Spain's past. These iconic locations offer a glimpse into the city's royal heritage, its role in the Spanish Empire, and its evolution over the centuries. Here are some of the must-visit historical sites and landmarks in Madrid:

1. The Royal Palace of Madrid (Palacio Real)

The Royal Palace of Madrid is one of the city's most impressive and iconic landmarks. Built in the 18th century on the site of a former Moorish fortress, it is the official residence of the Spanish Royal Family, although it is only used for state ceremonies today. The palace is the largest in Western Europe, with over 3,400 rooms, many of which are open to the public. Visitors can explore the grand halls, lavishly decorated with artwork, tapestries, and ornate furnishings, and admire the Throne Room, the Royal Armory, and the Royal Chapel. The palace gardens, including the Sabatini Gardens and Campo del Moro, offer stunning views and a peaceful retreat from the city's hustle and bustle.

2. Plaza Mayor

Plaza Mayor is the historic heart of Madrid and one of the city's most famous squares. Originally constructed in the early 17th century under King Philip III, whose statue dominates the center of the square, Plaza Mayor has been the site of numerous public events, from bullfights to markets and executions during the Spanish Inquisition. The square is surrounded by uniform, three-story buildings with charming balconies, and its arcades are lined with shops, cafes, and restaurants. Plaza Mayor is a popular gathering spot for both locals and tourists, offering a vibrant atmosphere and a glimpse into Madrid's historical significance.

3. Puerta del Sol

Puerta del Sol is another key landmark in Madrid, often considered the very center of Spain. This bustling square is where you'll find the famous "Kilometer Zero" plaque, marking the point from which all Spanish roads are measured. It's also home to the iconic statue of the Bear and the Strawberry Tree (El Oso y el Madroño), the symbol of Madrid. Puerta del Sol has been the site of many significant events in Spanish history, including the proclamation of the Second Republic in 1931 and the uprisings against French rule in 1808. Today, it's a popular meeting place and a hub of activity, especially on New Year's Eve when locals and visitors gather to ring in the new year.

4. Almudena Cathedral

Adjacent to the Royal Palace, Almudena Cathedral (Catedral de la Almudena) is Madrid's most important religious building. Although construction began in the late 19th century, the cathedral was not completed until 1993, when it was consecrated by Pope John Paul II. The cathedral's architecture is a blend of styles, with a neoclassical exterior that complements the Royal Palace and a modern, neo-Gothic interior. The crypt, however, dates back to the original construction period and features a stunning 16th-century altarpiece. Visitors can also climb to the cathedral's dome for panoramic views of Madrid.

5. El Escorial

While not located within the city itself, El Escorial is one of Spain's most significant historical sites and is easily accessible from Madrid as a day trip. This vast complex, located about 45 kilometers northwest of Madrid, was commissioned by King Philip II in the 16th century as a royal palace, monastery, and burial site for Spanish monarchs. El Escorial is a masterpiece of Renaissance architecture, with its austere design symbolizing the power and piety of the Spanish Empire. The complex includes the Royal Pantheon, where many Spanish kings and queens are interred, the

Basilica, with its impressive altarpiece, and a library housing thousands of priceless manuscripts. El Escorial's significance and grandeur make it a must-visit for history enthusiasts.

6. The Temple of Debod

One of Madrid's more unique historical landmarks is the Temple of Debod, an ancient Egyptian temple dating back to the 2nd century BC. This temple was gifted to Spain by the Egyptian government in 1968, in gratitude for Spain's help in saving the temples of Abu Simbel during the construction of the Aswan Dam. The temple was carefully reconstructed in Madrid's Parque del Oeste, near Plaza de España. Surrounded by a reflecting pool, the Temple of Debod offers a serene and picturesque spot, especially at sunset. It's a fascinating reminder of ancient history in the heart of modern Madrid.

7. The Prado Museum

While primarily known as one of the world's greatest art museums, the Prado Museum (Museo del Prado) is also a significant historical landmark. Opened in 1819, the museum's neoclassical building was originally designed as a natural history museum under King Charles III. Today, it houses one of the finest collections of European art, with masterpieces by Velázquez, Goya, Rubens, and Titian, among others. The Prado is not only a treasure trove of art but also a symbol of Spain's cultural heritage and its influence in the world of fine arts.

8. The Royal Basilica of San Francisco el Grande
This neoclassical basilica, located in the La Latina district, is one of Madrid's most impressive religious sites. Built in the late 18th century, the Royal Basilica of San Francisco el Grande is known for its massive dome, one of the largest in the world, and its stunning interior, which features artwork by notable Spanish artists, including Goya. The basilica's six chapels are adorned with elaborate altars, sculptures, and paintings, making it a must-see for those interested in religious art and architecture.

These historical sites and landmarks are just a glimpse of Madrid's rich heritage. Each offers a unique perspective on the city's past, from its royal legacy to its role as a cultural and political center. Exploring these sites provides a deeper understanding of Madrid's history and its enduring significance in Spain and beyond.

Museums and Art Galleries

Madrid is a cultural capital renowned for its incredible array of museums and art galleries, which house some of the most significant works of art and historical artifacts in the world. Whether you're an art enthusiast or a casual visitor, Madrid's museums offer a rich and diverse experience that reflects the city's deep artistic heritage and its role as a cultural hub. Here are some of the top museums and art galleries in Madrid, along with their locations:

1. **The Prado Museum (Museo del Prado)**
   - Location: Calle de Ruiz de Alarcón, 23, 28014 Madrid

The Prado Museum is Madrid's most famous and prestigious art museum, and one of the most significant in the world. Founded in 1819, the Prado is home to an unparalleled collection of European art from the 12th to the early 20th century. The museum's highlights include masterpieces by Spanish artists such as Velázquez, Goya, and El Greco, as well as works by other European masters like Rubens, Titian, and Bosch. Key pieces to see include Velázquez's Las Meninas, Goya's The Third of May 1808, and Bosch's The Garden of Earthly Delights. The Prado's vast collection, housed in a stunning neoclassical building, makes it an essential destination for art lovers.

2. **The Reina Sofía Museum (Museo Nacional Centro de Arte Reina Sofía)**
- **Location: Calle de Santa Isabel, 52, 28012 Madrid**

For those interested in modern and contemporary art, the Reina Sofía Museum is a must-visit. Opened in 1992 in a former hospital building, the museum is best known for its collection of 20th-century Spanish art, particularly works by Pablo Picasso and Salvador Dalí. The crown jewel of the Reina Sofía is Picasso's Guernica, a powerful anti-war painting that stands as one of the most iconic artworks of the 20th century. The museum also features works by Miró, Juan Gris, and other leading artists of the modernist movement. In addition to its permanent collection, the Reina Sofía hosts temporary exhibitions, offering a dynamic experience for visitors.

3. The Thyssen-Bornemisza Museum (Museo Nacional Thyssen-Bornemisza)
- Location: Paseo del Prado, 8, 28014 Madrid

The Thyssen-Bornemisza Museum completes Madrid's "Golden Triangle of Art," alongside the Prado and Reina Sofía. This museum offers a comprehensive overview of European art from the 13th century to the late 20th century. The collection, originally assembled by the Thyssen-Bornemisza family, includes works by artists such as Van Gogh, Caravaggio, Rembrandt, Monet, and Hopper. The museum's diverse range of styles and periods, from Renaissance and Baroque to Impressionism and Pop Art, makes it a perfect complement to the Prado and Reina Sofía. The Thyssen-Bornemisza's collection is housed in a beautiful neoclassical building on Paseo del Prado, providing an intimate setting for viewing these masterpieces.

4. The Royal Academy of Fine Arts of San Fernando (Real Academia de Bellas Artes de San Fernando)
- **Location: Calle de Alcalá, 13, 28014 Madrid**

Founded in 1744, the Royal Academy of Fine Arts of San Fernando is one of Spain's most important cultural institutions. The academy's museum boasts a rich collection of paintings, sculptures, and decorative arts spanning several centuries. It includes works by masters like Goya, Zurbarán, and Murillo. The museum is also notable for its collection of works by Francisco de Goya, who was both a student and a director of the academy. In addition to its permanent collection, the academy hosts temporary exhibitions and events that celebrate both historical and contemporary art.

5. The Sorolla Museum (Museo Sorolla)
- **Location: Calle General Martínez Campos, 37, 28010 Madrid**

Located in the former home and studio of the Spanish painter Joaquín Sorolla, the Sorolla Museum offers a more personal and intimate museum experience. Sorolla, known for his luminous and vibrant depictions of Mediterranean scenes, is one of Spain's most beloved artists. The museum's collection includes many of Sorolla's masterpieces, as well as his personal belongings, sketches, and letters. The house itself, preserved much as it was during Sorolla's life, provides insight into the artist's world and creative process. The museum also features a beautiful garden, designed by Sorolla, which adds to the charm of the visit.

6. The National Archaeological Museum (Museo Arqueológico Nacional)
- Location: Calle de Serrano, 13, 28001 Madrid

For history enthusiasts, the National Archaeological Museum is a treasure trove of artifacts that span Spain's rich and diverse history. The museum's extensive collection covers prehistoric times, the Roman and Islamic periods, the Middle Ages, and beyond. Notable exhibits include the Lady of Elche, an iconic Iberian sculpture, and the Visigothic crowns from the Treasure of Guarrazar. The museum also offers insights into the history of other cultures, with Egyptian, Greek, and Roman artifacts on display. The National Archaeological Museum, housed in a grand 19th-century building, provides a fascinating journey through Spain's past.

7. The Cerralbo Museum (Museo Cerralbo)
- Location: Calle de Ventura Rodríguez, 17, 28008 Madrid

The Cerralbo Museum is one of Madrid's lesser-known gems, offering a glimpse into the life of Spanish nobility in the late 19th century. The museum is housed in the lavish mansion of the Marquis of Cerralbo, a passionate collector of art and antiquities. The collection includes paintings, sculptures, ceramics, and armor, displayed in the opulent rooms of the mansion, which have been preserved in their original state. The Cerralbo Museum offers a unique experience, combining art, history, and the grandeur of aristocratic life.

8. The CaixaForum Madrid
Location: Paseo del Prado, 36, 28014 Madrid

CaixaForum Madrid is a modern cultural center housed in a striking contemporary building that features a vertical garden on its façade. The center hosts a wide range of temporary exhibitions, covering topics from classical art to contemporary photography and design. In addition to its exhibitions, CaixaForum offers cultural activities such as lectures, concerts, and workshops, making it a vibrant part of Madrid's cultural scene. Its location on Paseo del Prado, near other major museums, makes it a convenient stop on a cultural tour of the city.

9. The Museum of Romanticism (Museo del Romanticismo)
Location: Calle de San Mateo, 13, 28004 Madrid

The Museum of Romanticism transports visitors to 19th-century Madrid, offering a fascinating look at the Romantic period through art, furniture, and everyday objects. The museum is housed in a beautifully restored mansion and includes works by Goya, Madrazo, and Esquivel, among others. The collection also features period costumes, decorative arts, and a recreated 19th-century cafe. The museum's tranquil garden and charming tea room provide a perfect setting to relax after exploring the exhibits.

10. The Lázaro Galdiano Museum (Museo Lázaro Galdiano)
Location: Calle de Serrano, 122, 28006 Madrid
The Lázaro Galdiano Museum is a lesser-known but richly rewarding museum that houses the private collection of financier and philanthropist José Lázaro Galdiano. The museum's diverse collection includes paintings, sculptures, jewelry, and manuscripts, with works by Goya, Bosch, and El Greco, among others. The museum is located in the former residence of Lázaro Galdiano, a palatial mansion that adds to the allure of the visit. The Lázaro Galdiano Museum offers an intimate and eclectic museum experience, showcasing the passion and discerning taste of its founder.

Madrid's museums and art galleries offer a rich tapestry of artistic and historical experiences, reflecting the city's deep cultural roots and its ongoing role as a center of creativity and innovation. Whether you're drawn to the masterpieces of the Prado, the modernist icons of the Reina Sofía, or the personal collections of Madrid's aristocracy, these institutions provide a fascinating journey through the world of art and history.

Parks and Gardens

Madrid is a city where the pulse of urban life harmonizes with serene green spaces, offering locals and visitors a perfect blend of excitement and relaxation. From grand, historic parks to hidden botanical gems, Madrid's parks and gardens are vital oases that invite exploration, reflection, and recreation.

1. El Retiro Park
Location: Plaza de la Independencia, 7, 28001 Madrid

El Retiro Park is the crown jewel of Madrid's green spaces. Spanning over 125 hectares, this historic park is a haven for relaxation and cultural exploration. Visitors can row boats on the picturesque lake, admire art exhibitions in the Crystal Palace, and stroll through the beautifully landscaped gardens, including the iconic Rosaleda (rose garden). It's a must-visit for anyone wanting to experience Madrid's natural beauty and vibrant cultural scene.

2. Casa de Campo
Location: Paseo Puerta del Ángel, 1, 28011 Madrid
Madrid's largest park, Casa de Campo, offers a vast expanse of nature and recreation. Covering

over 1,700 hectares, this park includes a lake perfect for boating, extensive trails for hiking and cycling, and attractions like the Madrid Zoo and Amusement Park. Whether you're looking to explore or simply unwind, Casa de Campo provides an immersive natural retreat right within the city.

3. Sabatini Gardens
Location: Calle de Bailén, 2, 28013 Madrid

Nestled beside the Royal Palace, the Sabatini Gardens offer a serene escape in the heart of Madrid. These neoclassical gardens are perfect for a quiet afternoon stroll, with their symmetrical design, reflecting pools, and lush greenery providing a peaceful contrast to the grandeur of the adjacent palace. It's an ideal spot to soak in the historical atmosphere of Madrid.

4. Parque del Oeste
Location: Paseo de Moret, 2, 28008 Madrid

Parque del Oeste is a picturesque park known for its winding paths, lush landscapes, and cultural landmarks. The highlight is the Temple of Debod, an ancient Egyptian temple gifted to Spain, offering spectacular sunset views. The park's rose garden, La Rosaleda, is a must-see, especially in spring when thousands of roses are in bloom.

5. Madrid Río
Location: Along the Manzanares River, 28005 Madrid

Madrid Río is a vibrant, linear park stretching along the Manzanares River. This modern green space is perfect for biking, jogging, or a leisurely walk along the riverbanks. The park features playgrounds, sports facilities, and cultural centers like Matadero Madrid, making it a lively and dynamic part of the city.

6. Royal Botanical Garden
Location: Plaza de Murillo, 2, 28014 Madrid
Situated next to the Prado Museum, the Royal Botanical Garden is a tranquil oasis in the city center. With over 5,000 species of plants from around the world, beautifully arranged in terraced gardens, this space is perfect for plant lovers and those seeking a peaceful retreat. Seasonal flower displays and a stunning bonsai collection add to its charm.

Cultural Experiences in Madrid

Madrid bursts with cultural vitality, offering a captivating array of experiences that reflect its dynamic heritage and modern spirit. From the fiery passion of flamenco to vibrant festivals and a thriving performing arts scene, the city's cultural landscape is a celebration of tradition and innovation.

Flamenco: The Heartbeat of Spanish Culture

Experience the soul-stirring essence of flamenco, a quintessential Spanish art form that melds singing (cante), guitar playing (toque), and dancing (baile) into a powerful performance. Corral de la Morería, one of the city's most renowned tablaos, provides an authentic and immersive flamenco experience with nightly performances that showcase exceptional talent. For a more intimate setting, Casa Patas and Cardamomo offer captivating shows where the rhythms and emotions of flamenco come alive. Witnessing these performers is an unforgettable way to connect with the deep-rooted traditions of Spanish music and dance.

Festivals: A Feast for the Senses

Madrid's festival calendar is packed with events that highlight the city's exuberance and cultural diversity. San Isidro, celebrated in mid-May, transforms the city into a lively spectacle with traditional music, dance, parades, and bullfights. The festival's festive atmosphere extends to open-air concerts and fairs, creating a vibrant celebration of Madrid's heritage.

In late June and early July, Madrid Pride (Orgullo) takes center stage as one of the world's largest LGBTQ+ celebrations. This colorful event features a grand parade, parties, and cultural activities, turning Madrid into a dazzling display of inclusivity and joy.

The Three Kings Parade (Cabalgata de Reyes) on January 5th is a highlight for families, featuring elaborate floats, lively music, and performers that bring the story of the Three Wise Men to life. This enchanting parade marks the beginning of Epiphany celebrations and adds a touch of magic to the city's festive season.

Performing Arts: A Rich Tapestry of Talent
Madrid's performing arts scene offers something for everyone, from classical opera to cutting-edge contemporary theater. Teatro Real, the city's

grand opera house, provides an exceptional venue for experiencing both classic and modern operas in an opulent setting. For theater enthusiasts, Teatro Español and Teatro Lara are must-visits, showcasing a blend of traditional Spanish plays, contemporary productions, and international works.

To experience the uniquely Spanish art form of zarzuela, head to Teatro de la Zarzuela, where melodious performances blend operatic and popular music.

For those interested in contemporary and avant-garde performances, Teatros del Canal and Matadero Madrid offer dynamic programs of modern dance and innovative theatrical productions, reflecting the city's cutting-edge artistic spirit.

Cultural Diversity: A Global Crossroads
Madrid's cultural centers, such as CentroCentro and La Casa Encendida, provide a vibrant array of exhibitions, concerts, and workshops that celebrate the city's cosmopolitan character. Madrid Fusion, an annual culinary event, positions the city as a global gastronomic hub, where renowned chefs from around the world present the

latest in culinary creativity. The Festival de Otoño further enriches the cultural landscape with international theater, dance, and music performances, highlighting Madrid's role as a crossroads of global artistic exchange.

From the pulsating rhythms of flamenco to the grandeur of its festivals and the richness of its performing arts, Madrid offers a cultural experience that captivates and inspires. Each facet of the city's cultural life provides an opportunity to engage deeply with its vibrant spirit and creative energy.

CHAPTER THREE
Where To Stay And Getting Around

Best Neighborhoods to Stay in Madrid

Selecting the perfect neighborhood in Madrid can significantly enhance your travel experience. Each district offers its own unique charm, from historical streets to modern hubs, catering to various tastes and preferences. Here's a guide to some of the best neighborhoods in Madrid, ensuring a memorable stay tailored to your interests.

1. Sol and Gran Vía: The Heart of Madrid

Overview: Sol and Gran Vía are the quintessential centers of Madrid, pulsating with activity and brimming with attractions. Perfect for those who want to be at the epicenter of the city's excitement, these areas offer convenient access to major landmarks, shopping, and dining.

Highlights:
- ❖ **Attractions:** Explore the bustling Puerta del Sol (Sol, Madrid 28013), the iconic Plaza Mayor (Plaza Mayor, Madrid 28012), and the impressive Royal Palace (Calle Bailén,

Madrid 28071). Gran Vía (Gran Vía, Madrid 28013) is renowned for its theaters and grand architecture.
- **Dining:** A plethora of dining options from tapas bars to international restaurants.
- **Stay Options:** High-end hotels like Hotel Atlántico (Gran Vía, 38, Madrid 28013) and modern apartments in the area.
- **Why Stay Here:** Ideal for first-time visitors who want to be close to Madrid's top sights and enjoy vibrant nightlife.

2. Malasaña: Trendy and Bohemian

Overview: Malasaña is Madrid's bohemian enclave, known for its youthful energy, street art, and eclectic mix of boutiques and cafes. This neighborhood exudes a creative and lively atmosphere, attracting a diverse crowd.

Highlights:
- **Attractions:** Discover unique street art and quirky vintage shops around Plaza del Dos de Mayo (Plaza del Dos de Mayo, Madrid 28004) and the surrounding streets.
- **Dining:** Trendy cafes and artisanal eateries, such as Ouh Babushka (Calle de la Palma, 21, Madrid 28015) and La Ardosa (Calle de Colón, 13, Madrid 28004).

- **Stay Options:** Boutique hotels like Hotel 7 Islas (Calle de Valverde, 14, Madrid 28004) and charming guesthouses.
- **Why Stay Here:** Perfect for travelers who enjoy a vibrant, artistic vibe and want to experience Madrid's alternative culture.

3. La Latina: Historic and Charming

Overview: La Latina offers a glimpse into traditional Madrid with its narrow streets, historic buildings, and lively markets. Known for its authentic tapas bars and historic charm, this neighborhood is ideal for those seeking a more local experience.

Highlights:

- **Attractions:** Visit the famous El Rastro flea market (Calle de la Ribera de Curtidores, Madrid 28005) on Sundays and explore historic sites such as the Basilica of San Francisco el Grande (Calle de San Buenaventura, 1, Madrid 28005).
- **Dining:** A variety of traditional tapas bars and local eateries along the bustling Cava Baja (Cava Baja, Madrid 28005) street.
- **Stay Options:** Cozy inns and historic hotels like Posada del León de Oro (Cava Baja, 12, Madrid 28005).

- ❖ **Why Stay Here:** Great for those wanting to experience Madrid's traditional side and enjoy authentic Spanish cuisine.

4. Salamanca: Upscale and Sophisticated

<u>Overview</u>: Salamanca is synonymous with luxury and elegance. Known for its high-end shopping, upscale dining, and refined atmosphere, this neighborhood is perfect for travelers seeking a more sophisticated experience.

Highlights:
- ❖ **Attractions:** Stroll down Calle Serrano (Calle Serrano, Madrid 28001) for high-end shopping, visit the Museo Lázaro Galdiano (Calle de Serrano, 122, Madrid 28006), and enjoy the refined architecture of the area.
- ❖ **Dining:** Gourmet restaurants and chic cafes, such as Ramses.Life (Plaza de la República del Ecuador, 2, Madrid 28016) and Sergi Arola Gastro (Calle de Zurbano, 31, Madrid 28010).
- ❖ **Stay Options:** Luxury hotels like Hotel Wellington (Calle de Velázquez, 8, Madrid 28001) and upscale apartments.
- ❖ **Why Stay Here:** Ideal for those who appreciate luxury, premium shopping, and a stylish environment.

5. Chamberí: Elegant and Residential

Overview: Chamberí is a charming, residential neighborhood that combines elegance with a relaxed vibe. Its tree-lined streets and beautiful architecture offer a more tranquil retreat from the bustling city center.

Highlights:
- **Attractions:** Explore the Museo Sorolla (Paseo del General Martínez Campos, 37, Madrid 28010) and the lovely Parque de Chamberí (Parque de Chamberí, Madrid 28010). The area also features a variety of local shops and cafes.
- **Dining:** Classic Spanish restaurants and cozy cafes, such as La Sastrería (Calle de Vallehermoso, 79, Madrid 28015).
- **Stay Options:** Elegant hotels like Hotel Orfila (Calle de Orfila, 6, Madrid 28010) and comfortable vacation rentals.
- **Why Stay Here:** Suited for travelers seeking a quieter, more residential experience with easy access to central attractions.

6. Retiro: Relaxed and Scenic

Overview: Adjacent to El Retiro Park, the Retiro neighborhood offers a serene escape with scenic green spaces and a peaceful atmosphere. Perfect for those who enjoy outdoor activities and a relaxed pace.

Highlights:
- ❖ **Attractions:** Enjoy the vast green spaces of El Retiro Park (Plaza de la Independencia, 7, Madrid 28001), visit the Crystal Palace (Parque del Retiro, Madrid 28009), and explore the nearby Prado Museum (Calle de Ruiz de Alarcón, 23, Madrid 28014).
- ❖ **Dining:** Relaxed cafes and casual dining options, such as La Cocina de María Luisa (Calle del Doctor Castelo, 5, Madrid 28009).
- ❖ **Stay Options:** Boutique hotels and comfortable rentals near the park, such as Petit Palace Santa Bárbara (Calle de las Hortensias, 1, Madrid 28002).
- ❖ **Why Stay Here:** Ideal for families, nature lovers, and anyone seeking a peaceful retreat with easy access to cultural sites.

Each of these neighborhoods in Madrid offers a distinct experience, allowing you to tailor your stay to match your interests and preferences. Whether you're drawn to the vibrant city center, the artistic energy of Malasaña, or the tranquil beauty of Retiro, Madrid has a neighborhood that's just right for you.

Accommodation Options in Madrid

Luxury Accommodations
1. Gran Meliá Palacio de los Duques

- **Cost per Night:** €400−€800
- **Website:** [Gran Meliá Palacio de los Duques](https://www.melia.com)
- **Call:** +34 912 764 747
- **Location:** Cuesta de Santo Domingo 5, 28013 Madrid

Overview: A 5-star hotel located near the Royal Palace, offering luxury in a historic setting. The hotel is a former 19th-century palace with

48

beautifully manicured gardens and elegant interiors.

How to Get There: Take Metro Line 2 or 5 to Ópera station. The hotel is a 5-minute walk from the station.

Room Features:
- Luxuriously decorated rooms with marble bathrooms
- Nespresso machines, flat-screen TVs, high-quality linens
- Suites with private terraces and views of the Royal Palace

Amenities:
- Rooftop pool with panoramic views
- Full-service Clarins Spa and fitness center
- Concierge services

Dining Options:
- **Dos Cielos Madrid:** Michelin-starred restaurant
- **Montmartre 1889:** French-inspired brasserie

Unique Features:
- Historical art collection
- Afternoon tea in the palace's garden

2. The Westin Palace Madrid

- **Cost per Night:** €350–€700
- **Website:**[The Westin Palace Madrid](https://www.marriott.com)
- **Call:** +34 913 608 000
- **Location:** Plaza de las Cortes 7, 28014 Madrid

Overview: A historic 5-star hotel known for its Belle Époque architecture, located near the Prado Museum. Famous for its opulent interior and grand glass dome.

How to Get There: Metro Line 2 to Banco de España station. A 5-minute walk to the hotel.

Room Features:
- Spacious rooms with Westin's signature Heavenly Beds
- Marble bathrooms, flat-screen TVs, and minibars
- Suites offer separate living areas and balconies

Amenities:
- Full-service wellness center and spa
- 24-hour fitness center
- Business center and meeting rooms

Dining Options:
- **La Rotonda:** Mediterranean cuisine under the hotel's famous glass dome
- **Asia Gallery:** Asian fusion cuisine

Unique Features:
- Glass dome where afternoon tea is served
- Hosted famous guests, including royalty

3. Hotel Ritz by Mandarin Oriental
- **Cost per Night:** €500–€1,200
- **Website:** [Hotel Ritz] (https://www.mandarinoriental.com)
- **Call:** +34 917 016 767

- **Location:** Plaza de la Lealtad 5, 28014 Madrid

Overview: A grand 5-star hotel built in 1910, located near the Prado Museum. Known for its old-world charm and luxurious amenities.

How to Get There: Metro Line 1 to Atocha station. The hotel is a 10-minute walk from the station.

Room Features:
- Classic décor with luxury linens and marble bathrooms
- Suites with separate dining areas and butler service
- Views of the Prado Museum or the hotel's lush garden

Amenities:
- ❖ Rooftop fitness center and outdoor terraces
- ❖ Full-service spa and wellness center
- ❖ Concierge services with private tours

Dining Options:
- ❖ **Deessa:** Michelin-starred restaurant by Chef Quique Dacosta
- ❖ **Palm Court:** High tea and afternoon drinks

Unique Features:
- ❖ Historic architecture and fine art collection
- ❖ Exclusive luxury services like personal shoppers

4. Four Seasons Hotel Madrid

- Cost per Night: €550–€1,500
- **Website:** [Four Seasons Madrid]. (https://www.fourseasons.com)
- Call: +34 910 883 333
- **Location:** Calle de Sevilla 3, 28014 Madrid

Overview: Located in a newly restored historic building, the Four Seasons Madrid offers a luxurious retreat in the heart of Madrid's shopping and cultural district.

How to Get There: Metro Line 2 to Sevilla station. The hotel is right next to the station.

Room Features:
- Spacious, elegantly designed rooms with marble bathrooms
- High-end linens, flat-screen TVs, Nespresso machines
- Suites offer city views and private terraces

Amenities:
- Rooftop pool and bar with stunning views
- Full-service spa, offering signature Four Seasons treatments
- Fitness center and luxury shops on-site

Dining Options:
- **Dani:** Rooftop restaurant by Michelin-starred chef Dani García

- ❖ **El Patio:** All-day dining in a sun-filled atrium

Unique Features:
- ❖ Rooftop bar with 360-degree city views
- ❖ On-site luxury boutiques and personal shopping services

5. VP Plaza España Design

- ❖ **Cost per Night:** €300–€500
- ❖ **Website:** [VP Plaza España Design](https://www.vphoteles.com)
- ❖ **Call:** +34 915 953 490
- ❖ **Location:** Plaza de España 5, 28008 Madrid

Overview: This sleek, modern hotel located on the iconic Plaza de España offers contemporary design

and luxury amenities, including a unique vertical garden.
How to Get There: Metro Line 3 or 10 to Plaza de España station. The hotel is right on the square.

Room Features:
- ❖ Modern rooms with panoramic views and state-of-the-art technology
- ❖ Floor-to-ceiling windows, Nespresso machines, and designer bathrooms
- ❖ Suites with separate living areas and large terraces

Amenities:
- ❖ Rooftop bar and infinity pool
- ❖ Full-service wellness center and gym
- ❖ Event spaces and meeting rooms

Dining Options:
- ❖ **Ginkgo Sky Bar:** Rooftop bar with Mediterranean cuisine and cocktails
- ❖ **Botania:** Elegant indoor garden restaurant offering international dishes

Unique Features:
- ❖ Rooftop infinity pool with city views
- ❖ Vertical garden spanning several floors

Mid-Range/Boutique Accommodations
1. Hotel Urban

- ❖ **Cost per Night:** €250–€400
- ❖ **Website:** [Hotel Urban] (https://www.derbyhotels.com)
- ❖ **Call:** +34 917 877 770
- ❖ **Location:** Carrera de San Jerónimo 34, 28014 Madrid

Overview: A chic, art-filled boutique hotel near Puerta del Sol, Hotel Urban offers modern luxury with a contemporary design, perfect for art lovers.

How to Get There: Metro Line 2 to Sevilla station. The hotel is a 3-minute walk away.

Room Features:

- Modern, minimalist design with marble bathrooms
- Smart TVs, Nespresso machines, and in-room art collections
- Suites offer separate living areas and terraces

Amenities:
- Rooftop pool with a trendy bar
- Art gallery within the hotel featuring African and Asian art
- 24-hour fitness center

Dining Options:
- **CEBO:** Michelin-starred restaurant offering creative Spanish cuisine
- **Glass Mar:** A trendy bar offering cocktails and seafood dishes

Unique Features:
- In-house art gallery showcasing international antiquities
- Rooftop terrace with panoramic city views

2. Only YOU Boutique Hotel
- **Cost per Night:** €180–€350
- **Website:** [Only YOU Boutique Hotel] (https://www.onlyyouhotels.com)

- **Call:** +34 910 052 746
- **Location:** Calle Barquillo 21, 28004 Madrid

Overview: A stylish boutique hotel in Chueca, Only YOU Boutique Hotel offers an elegant, eclectic design perfect for couples and leisure travelers.

How to Get There: Metro Line 5 to Chueca station. A 5-minute walk to the hotel.

Room Features:
- Individually designed rooms with contemporary art and colorful accents
- Smart TVs, high-quality linens, and rainfall showers
- Suites feature balconies or terraces with city views

Amenities:
- Full-service spa with signature treatments
- Fitness center with state-of-the-art equipment
- Meeting rooms and event spaces

Dining Options:
- **YOUnique Restaurant:** Offering Mediterranean fusion cuisine
- **El Padrino:** An elegant bar with cocktails and light bites

Unique Features:
- ❖ Eclectic, art-filled interiors designed by famous Spanish interior designers
- ❖ Personal concierge services tailored to guests' needs

3. TÓTEM Madrid

- ❖ **Cost per Night:** €170–€300
- ❖ **Website:** [TÓTEM Madrid] (https://www.totem-madrid.com)
- ❖ **Call:** +34 912 172 762
- ❖ **Location:** Calle Hermosilla 23, 28001 Madrid

Overview: Located in Salamanca, this sleek boutique hotel offers minimalist design and a sophisticated atmosphere for those looking for a chic stay in Madrid's upscale district.

How to Get There: Metro Line 4 to Serrano station. The hotel is a 5-minute walk away.

Room Features:
- ❖ Stylish, modern rooms with wooden floors and marble bathrooms
- ❖ Smart TVs, plush linens, and luxury bath products
- ❖ Suites with separate living rooms and city views

Amenities:
- ❖ Full-service fitness center
- ❖ In-room massage and spa services available
- ❖ Meeting rooms for business travelers

Dining Options:
- ❖ **Hermosos y Malditos:** A chic restaurant and bar serving Mediterranean and fusion cuisine

Unique Features:
- ❖ Located in the exclusive Salamanca shopping district
- ❖ Personal trainers available upon request

4. **Dear Hotel Madrid**
   - ❖ **Cost per Night**: €150–€300
   - ❖ **Website:** [Dear Hotel Madrid] (https://dearhotelmadrid.com)
   - ❖ **Call:** +34 913 526 800
   - ❖ **Location:** Gran Vía 80, 28013 Madrid

Overview: This boutique hotel is known for its stylish design and rooftop terrace with an infinity pool, offering stunning views of the Madrid skyline.

How to Get There: Metro Line 10 to Plaza de España station. The hotel is a 2-minute walk away.

Room Features:
- ❖ Sleek rooms with neutral tones and floor-to-ceiling windows
- ❖ Nespresso machines, flat-screen TVs, and rainfall showers
- ❖ Some suites offer private terraces with panoramic views

Amenities:
- ❖ Rooftop infinity pool with city views
- ❖ 24-hour concierge services
- ❖ Meeting and event spaces

Dining Options:
- ❖ Nice to Meet You: Rooftop restaurant offering Mediterranean cuisine and cocktails

Unique Features:
- ❖ Rooftop infinity pool and restaurant with stunning views of Madrid.

5. Hotel Preciados

- ❖ **Cost per Night:** €120–€250
- ❖ Website: [Hotel Preciados] (https://www.hotelpreciados.com)
- ❖ Call: +34 915 237 980
- ❖ **Location:** Calle Preciados 37, 28013 Madrid

Overview: A centrally located boutique hotel near Puerta del Sol, offering stylish, comfortable rooms and excellent amenities.

How to Get There: Metro Line 1, 2, or 3 to Sol station. A 5-minute walk to the hotel.

Room Features:
- Modern rooms with wood floors and marble bathrooms
- Free minibar, flat-screen TVs, and in-room safes
- Suites with separate living areas and balconies

Amenities:
- 24-hour room service and concierge
- Free Wi-Fi and business center
- Fitness center

Dining Options:
- **Café Varela:** Offering Spanish and Mediterranean cuisine in a historic setting

Unique Features:
- Centrally located, close to major landmarks like Puerta del Sol and Gran Vía
- Complimentary minibar stocked daily

Budget Accommodations
1. Generator Madrid
- ❖ **Cost per Night**: €25–€120 (Dormitories and Private Rooms)
- ❖ **Website:** [Generator Madrid] (https://staygenerator.com)
- ❖ **Call:** +34 910 470 392
- ❖ **Location:** Calle de San Bernardo 2, 28013 Madrid

Overview: A trendy hostel offering modern design, social spaces, and an energetic atmosphere, Generator Madrid is perfect for young travelers and backpackers.

How to Get There: Metro Line 1 or 5 to Gran Vía station. A 3-minute walk to the hostel.

Room Features:
- ❖ Shared dormitories with individual lighting, USB outlets, and lockers
- ❖ Private rooms with en-suite bathrooms
- ❖ Free Wi-Fi and modern decor throughout

Amenities:
- ❖ Rooftop terrace with lounge seating
- ❖ On-site café and bar
- ❖ 24-hour reception and social events like walking tours and pub crawls

Dining Options:
- On-site café for breakfast and snacks
- Rooftop bar offering cocktails

Unique Features:
- Daily social events like pub crawls and live music
- Trendy rooftop terrace with city views

2. The Hat Madrid
- **Cost per Night:** €30–€100 (Dormitories and Private Rooms)
- **Website:** [The Hat Madrid] (https://thehatmadrid.com)
- **Call:** +34 917 728 572
- **Location:** Calle Imperial 9, 28012 Madrid

Overview: A stylish eco-friendly hostel in La Latina, The Hat Madrid offers a boutique experience with shared dormitories and private rooms.

How to Get There: Metro Line 5 to La Latina station. A 3-minute walk to the hostel.

Room Features:
- Shared dormitories with personal lockers, reading lights, and USB chargers

- ❖ Private rooms available with en-suite bathrooms
- ❖ Modern, minimalist design

Amenities:
- ❖ Rooftop bar and terrace with views of La Latina
- ❖ Free Wi-Fi, luggage storage, and bike rentals
- ❖ Social events like tapas nights and walking tours

Dining Options:
- ❖ Rooftop bar serving drinks and light bites

Unique Features:
- ❖ Eco-friendly design using renewable energy
- ❖ Rooftop terrace with city views

3. Room007 Chueca Hostel

- ❖ **Cost per Night:** €30–€100 (Dormitories and Private Rooms)
- ❖ **Website:** [Room007 Chueca Hostel] (https://www.room007.com)
- ❖ **Call:** +34 913 688 111
- ❖ **Location:** Calle de Hortaleza 74, 28004 Madrid

Overview: Located in the trendy Chueca neighborhood, Room007 Chueca Hostel offers modern, comfortable dormitories and private rooms at affordable rates.

How to Get There: Metro Line 1 to Chueca station. A 2-minute walk from the station.

Room Features:
- ❖ Shared dorms with personal lockers, reading lights, and USB chargers
- ❖ Private rooms available with en-suite bathrooms
- ❖ Simple, modern decor with vibrant colors

Amenities:
- ❖ Rooftop terrace with city views

- ❖ Shared kitchen and lounge area for guest use
- ❖ 24-hour front desk and luggage storage

Dining Options:
- ❖ **Saporem:** On-site restaurant serving Mediterranean-inspired dishes

Unique Features:
- ❖ Regular social activities like cooking classes and group dinners
- ❖ Trendy rooftop terrace with city views

4. OK Hostel Madrid

- **Cost per Night:** €25–€90 (Dormitories and Private Rooms)
- **Website:** [OK Hostel Madrid] (https://www.okhostelmadrid.com)
- **Call:** +34 914 202 709
- **Location:** Calle de Juanelo 24, 28012 Madrid

Overview: Located in the La Latina neighborhood, OK Hostel Madrid offers comfortable accommodations with a social, friendly atmosphere. It's perfect for budget-conscious travelers looking for a lively area.

How to Get There: Metro Line 1 or 5 to La Latina station. A 5-minute walk to the hostel.

Room Features:
- Shared dorms with lockers and individual reading lights
- Private rooms available for couples or small groups
- Modern, minimalist decor with colorful accents

Amenities:
- Shared kitchen and common lounge areas
- Free Wi-Fi and laundry facilities
- Daily events like walking tours and pub crawls

Dining Options:
- ❖ On-site bar offering breakfast and dinner

Unique Features:
- ❖ Social activities and events for travelers to meet and interact
- ❖ Close proximity to Madrid's best tapas bars

5. Bastardo Hostel

- ❖ **Cost per Night:** €30–€120 (Dormitories and Private Rooms)
- ❖ **Website:** [Bastardo Hostel] (https://bastardohostel.com)
- ❖ **Call:** +34 915 215 058
- ❖ **Location:** Calle de San Mateo 3, 28004 Madrid

Overview: A trendy, artsy hostel located in Malasaña, Bastardo Hostel features stylish, modern design with social spaces and a rooftop terrace, perfect for young travelers.

How to Get There: Metro Line 10 to Tribunal station. A 2-minute walk to the hostel.

Room Features:
- ❖ Shared dormitories with private lockers and curtains for privacy

- Private rooms with en-suite bathrooms for couples or families
- Chic, industrial-style decor

Amenities:
- Rooftop terrace with bar and seating
- On-site cinema and event space
- Free Wi-Fi and co-working space

Dining Options:
- **Limbo:** On-site restaurant serving grilled meats and local specialties

Unique Features:
- Regular live music, art exhibitions, and cinema screenings
- Industrial-chic decor and communal spaces for socializing

Vacation Rentals and Apartments

1. Eric Vökel Boutique Apartments – Madrid Suites
   - **Cost per Night:** €100–€250
   - **Website:** [Eric Vökel Apartments] (https://www.ericvokel.com)
   - **Call:** +34 911 829 635
   - **Location:** Calle de San Bernardo 61, 28015 Madrid

Overview: Eric Vökel Boutique Apartments offers stylish, Scandinavian-inspired vacation rentals in the vibrant Malasaña district. These fully-equipped apartments feature a blend of modern design and comfort, ideal for families and long-term stays.

How to Get There: Metro Line 1 or 10 to Tribunal station. The apartment is a 3-minute walk from the station.

Room Features:
- ❖ Fully equipped kitchens with modern appliances (oven, microwave, refrigerator)
- ❖ Spacious living rooms with flat-screen TVs and sofa beds
- ❖ Private balconies in select apartments
- ❖ One- to three-bedroom options, suitable for up to 6 guests

Amenities:
- Free Wi-Fi throughout the property
- In-room washer and dryer
- Reception desk with concierge services
- Housekeeping service available upon request

Unique Features:
- Stylish Scandinavian design with open layouts
- Eco-friendly apartment building with energy-efficient appliances
- Ideal location near bars, restaurants, and shopping in Malasaña

Dining Options:
- Fully equipped kitchen for preparing your own meals
- Located near popular local restaurants and tapas bars in Malasaña

2. Arenal Suites Gran Vía
- **Cost per Night:** €120–€250
- **Website:** [Arenal Suites Gran Vía](https://www.arenalsuites.com)
- **Call:** +34 910 053 570
- **Location:** Calle de la Salud 13, 28013 Madrid

Overview: Arenal Suites Gran Vía provides spacious, fully furnished apartments near Madrid's iconic Gran Vía. These modern, family-friendly suites offer a central location with easy access to shopping, dining, and Madrid's main attractions.

How to Get There: Metro Line 1 or 5 to Gran Vía station. A 2-minute walk from the station.

Room Features:
- Fully equipped kitchens with microwaves, stovetops, and dishwashers
- Comfortable living areas with flat-screen TVs and modern decor
- Two-bedroom and studio options, accommodating 2 to 5 guests
- Air-conditioning and heating

Amenities:
- ❖ Free Wi-Fi and flat-screen TVs
- ❖ Elevator access for convenience
- ❖ Laundry facilities on-site
- ❖ Concierge services for restaurant recommendations and tour bookings

Unique Features:
- ❖ Large family apartments in the heart of Madrid's busiest shopping district
- ❖ Daily housekeeping included
- ❖ Child-friendly with baby cots and high chairs available upon request

Dining Options:
- ❖ Fully equipped kitchen for self-catering
- ❖ Surrounded by excellent restaurants and cafes along Gran Vía and Puerta del Sol

3. Slow Suites Luchana
- ❖ **Cost per Night:** €110–€200
- ❖ **Website:** [Slow Suites] (https://www.slowsuites.com)
- ❖ **Call:** +34 914 446 112
- ❖ **Location:** Calle de Luchana 13, 28010 Madrid

Overview: Slow Suites Luchana offers modern apartments in the Chamberí district, known for its upscale charm and proximity to cultural attractions. The apartments feature minimalist design and are perfect for business travelers or couples.

How to Get There: Metro Line 1 to Bilbao station. The apartment is a 3-minute walk from the station.

Room Features:
- One- to two-bedroom apartments with open-concept living and dining areas
- Fully equipped kitchens with oven, stove, and dishwasher
- Hardwood floors, air-conditioning, and modern furnishings
- Smart TVs and free Wi-Fi

Amenities:
- Weekly cleaning service for long-term stays
- Elevator and secure entry
- Private parking available upon request
- Reception and tour assistance

Unique Features:
- Stylish, minimalist apartments with modern amenities

- Located in the elegant Chamberí neighborhood, close to theaters and galleries
- Ideal for both business and leisure travelers

Dining Options:
- Fully equipped kitchen for preparing meals
- Located near numerous high-end restaurants and traditional Spanish taverns in Chamberí

4. Apartosuites Jardines de Sabatini
- **Cost per Night:** €130–€220
- **Website:** [Jardines de Sabatini] (https://www.jardinesdesabatini.com)
- **Call:** +34 915 488 510
- **Location:** Cuesta de San Vicente 16, 28008 Madrid

Overview: Located near the Royal Palace, Apartosuites Jardines de Sabatini offers elegant apartments with hotel-like amenities. These apartments are designed for longer stays, making them an ideal choice for families or business travelers looking for space and comfort.

How to Get There: Metro Line 10 to Plaza de España station. A 5-minute walk to the property.

Room Features:
- One- and two-bedroom apartments with kitchenettes
- Living areas with sofa beds and flat-screen TVs
- City views from many apartments
- High-speed Wi-Fi and daily cleaning services

Amenities:
- Rooftop terrace with views of the Royal Palace
- 24-hour reception and concierge services
- On-site parking available
- Laundry services upon request

Unique Features:
- Stunning rooftop terrace with panoramic views of Madrid's Royal Palace
- Art gallery featuring vintage cars on-site
- Convenient access to major tourist attractions like Plaza de España and Gran Vía

Dining Options:
- Fully equipped kitchenette for self-catering
- Nearby restaurants offering traditional Spanish dishes and international cuisine

5. Madrid SmartRentals Chueca

- ❖ **Cost per Night:** €90–€180
- ❖ **Website:** [Madrid SmartRentals] (https://www.madridsmartrentals.com)
- ❖ **Call:** +34 915 217 710
- ❖ **Location:** Calle de San Marcos 8, 28004 Madrid

Overview: Madrid SmartRentals Chueca offers modern apartments in the trendy Chueca neighborhood, known for its lively atmosphere and cultural diversity. These apartments are a great option for solo travelers, couples, or groups wanting to explore Madrid's nightlife and food scene.

How to Get There: Metro Line 1 to Chueca station. A 2-minute walk from the station.

Room Features:
- ❖ One- to three-bedroom apartments with fully equipped kitchens
- ❖ Living areas with modern decor, sofa beds, and flat-screen TVs
- ❖ Air-conditioning and heating systems
- ❖ Free Wi-Fi and laundry facilities

Amenities:
- ❖ 24-hour concierge and reception service
- ❖ Airport transfer services available

- ❖ Weekly cleaning for long stays
- ❖ Elevator access and luggage storage

Unique Features:
- ❖ Located in one of Madrid's trendiest neighborhoods
- ❖ Pet-friendly apartments available upon request
- ❖ Short walking distance to popular spots like Gran Vía and Malasaña

Dining Options:
- ❖ Fully equipped kitchen for preparing meals
- ❖ Surrounded by chic cafes, tapas bars, and vibrant nightlife options in Chueca

Public Transportation and Getting Around Madrid

Madrid's extensive and efficient public transportation system makes navigating the city straightforward, offering various options for locals and tourists alike. Whether you're exploring the heart of the city or venturing further afield, here's a detailed guide to getting around Madrid using public transportation.

1. Metro: Fast and Efficient
The Madrid Metro is the backbone of the city's public transport system. With 13 lines covering over 300 stations, it's one of the most extensive metro networks in the world. The metro is perfect for quick trips across the city and reaching popular tourist spots.

- **Operating Hours**: 6:00 AM to 1:30 AM daily.
- **Ticket Prices:** A single ticket costs between €1.50 and €2.00, depending on the number of stops. A 10-trip ticket costs around €12.20, and a Tourist Travel Pass offers unlimited rides for 1 to 7 days, starting at €8.40.

Key Lines:
- Line 1 (Light Blue) connects Sol and Atocha, important city hubs.
- Line 3 (Yellow) runs through central stops like Moncloa and Lavapiés.
- Line 8 (Pink) links Madrid-Barajas Airport to Nuevos Ministerios.

2. EMT Buses: Exploring Above Ground

Madrid's EMT bus network features over 200 routes, providing an excellent complement to the metro. Buses are ideal for those who prefer above-ground travel, with routes covering the entire city.

- Operating Hours: Most buses run from 6:00 AM to 11:30 PM, with Night Buses (known as Búhos) operating from 11:30 PM to 6:00 AM.
- Ticket Prices: A single ticket costs €1.50, the same as the metro, and the Tourist Travel Pass covers buses as well.

Popular Routes:
- C1/C2 Circular Lines: Great for touring central Madrid, passing by iconic sights like Retiro Park and Prado Museum.
- Airport Express Bus: Operates 24/7 and connects Adolfo Suárez Madrid-Barajas

Airport to Atocha Station and other key stops for €5.

3. Cercanías Trains: For Day Trips and Suburbs

The Cercanías is Madrid's commuter rail system, run by Renfe, offering fast connections between the city center and surrounding towns, making it perfect for day trips.

- Main Stations: Major hubs include Atocha (Cercanías Lines C1, C2, etc.) and Chamartín.
- Destinations: Popular day-trip destinations include Toledo, Segovia, and El Escorial, all reachable within 30 to 60 minutes.
- Ticket Prices: Prices vary depending on distance, typically between €1.70 and €8 for trips within the Madrid area.

4. Taxis and Ride-Sharing: Convenient and Flexible

Taxis are widely available throughout Madrid, and ride-sharing apps like Uber and Cabify are also popular for a quick and comfortable way to travel.

- Taxi Fares: The base fare starts at around €3.50, with a flat rate of €30 for trips

between Madrid-Barajas Airport and the city center.
- Uber and Cabify: Both services offer competitive rates with easy-to-use apps, making it simple to request a ride anywhere in the city.

5. BiciMAD: Bike Rentals for Active Exploration

Madrid's BiciMAD electric bike rental system is an eco-friendly option for travelers who prefer exploring the city at their own pace. With numerous docking stations, it's a flexible way to get around, especially in the city center and parks.

- Cost: The first 30 minutes cost €2, with additional charges for longer usage. BiciMAD stations can be found at major points like Retiro Park, Plaza Mayor, and Gran Vía.
- Why Use It: Perfect for short rides around scenic areas like El Retiro Park or the historic Madrid Río park.

6. Walking: The Best Way to Explore Central Madrid

Many of Madrid's main attractions are within walking distance of each other, especially in the central districts. Walking allows visitors to experience the city's atmosphere, from the vibrant Gran Vía to the historical La Latina neighborhood.

Areas to Explore:
- Puerta del Sol to Plaza Mayor is a pleasant walk full of historical sites.
- Gran Vía to Calle de Serrano offers a mix of shopping and cultural landmarks like the Metropolis Building.

7. Adolfo Suárez Madrid-Barajas Airport: Getting to and from the City

Madrid's international airport is located just 12 km from the city center and is well connected by public transport.

- Metro: Line 8 takes you directly from Barajas Airport to the central Nuevos Ministerios station in about 15 minutes, with an airport surcharge of €3.
- Cercanías Train: The C1 train connects Terminal 4 with Atocha and Chamartín stations.
- Airport Express Bus: Running 24/7, this bus is another option for getting to and from the airport, with stops at Atocha and Plaza Cibeles.

Useful tips for Getting Around Madrid
1. Multi Card: Madrid's Multi Card is a reloadable card that works for all public transport. It's ideal for those who plan to stay longer or use a variety of transportation methods.
2. Tourist Travel Pass: For visitors, the Tourist Travel Pass offers unlimited access to metro, buses, and Cercanías trains for a set number of days (1 to 7 days), making it easy to explore Madrid without worrying about multiple tickets.
3. Parking: If driving, parking in central Madrid can be difficult and expensive, so public transport is often the better option.

CHAPTER FOUR
Madrid For Foodies And Shoppers

Must-Try Dishes and Top Restaurants in Madrid
Madrid's food scene is a delicious blend of traditional Spanish cuisine, innovative contemporary dishes, and international flavors. From savory tapas to indulgent desserts, the city offers a gastronomic experience that satisfies every palate. Here's a guide to the must-try dishes and the best places to enjoy them.

1. Must-Try Dishes in Madrid
1.1. Cocido Madrileño

This hearty, slow-cooked stew is Madrid's signature dish. Made with chickpeas, various cuts of pork, chorizo, morcilla (blood sausage), and vegetables, it's served in stages: first the broth, then the chickpeas and vegetables, and finally the meat.

Where to Try It: La Bola (Calle de la Bola, 5, Madrid 28013) – Known for its authentic and perfectly prepared cocido, cooked in traditional clay pots.

1.2. Bocadillo de Calamares (Calamari Sandwich)

A simple yet iconic Madrid snack, the bocadillo de calamares is a crispy fried calamari sandwich, typically served with a drizzle of lemon or alioli.

Where to Try It:
- El Brillante (Plaza del Emperador Carlos V, 8, Madrid 28012) – Famous for its fresh, perfectly fried calamari sandwiches, a must-visit near Atocha Station.
- La Campana (Calle de Botoneras, 6, Madrid 28012) – One of the most famous spots near Plaza Mayor for an authentic calamari sandwich experience.

1.3. Huevos Rotos

Literally meaning "broken eggs," this dish features fried eggs served over crispy potatoes, often accompanied by Iberian ham or chorizo. It's a popular comfort food in Madrid.

Where to Try It:

Casa Lucio (Calle de la Cava Baja, 35, Madrid 28005), Famous for serving some of the best huevos rotos in the city, it's a favorite of locals and celebrities alike.

1.4. Callos a la Madrileña

Another traditional Madrid dish, this rich and flavorful tripe stew is made with beef tripe, blood sausage, chorizo, and a thick tomato-based sauce.

It's a hearty meal often enjoyed in the colder months.

Where to Try It:

Lhardy (Carrera de San Jerónimo, 8, Madrid 28014), One of Madrid's most historic restaurants, Lhardy is renowned for its classic callos and old-world charm.

1.5. Tortilla Española (Spanish Omelette)
A staple in Spanish cuisine, this simple yet delicious dish is made from eggs, potatoes, and onions. Whether served as a tapa or a full meal, it's a must-try in Madrid.

Where to Try It:

Casa Dani (Mercado de la Paz, Calle de Ayala, 28, Madrid 28001), Considered one of the best places for a perfectly cooked tortilla in the city.

1.6. Churros con Chocolate
For dessert or a sweet snack, nothing beats churros with thick, rich hot chocolate. The crispy fried dough is dipped into the warm chocolate, making it a beloved treat in Madrid.

Where to Try It:

Chocolatería San Ginés (Pasadizo de San Ginés, 5, Madrid 28013) – The most famous place in Madrid for churros con chocolate, serving this indulgent treat since 1894.

2. Top Restaurants in Madrid

Madrid's dining scene ranges from traditional taverns to Michelin-starred restaurants, offering a culinary journey through Spain's flavors and beyond. Here are some top restaurants to check out:

2.1. DiverXO (3 Michelin Stars)

Location: Calle del Padre Damián, 23, Madrid 28036

Chef Dabiz Muñoz's DiverXO is Madrid's only three-Michelin-star restaurant, where avant-garde cuisine meets artistic presentations. The menu blends international influences with traditional Spanish flavors in a playful, sensory dining experience.

2.2. Sobrino de Botín (World's Oldest Restaurant)

Location: Calle de Cuchilleros, 17, Madrid 28005

Founded in 1725, Sobrino de Botín holds the Guinness World Record for being the oldest continuously operating restaurant in the world. Known for its cochinillo asado (roast suckling pig) and cordero asado (roast lamb), the restaurant is a step back in time and a Madrid dining institution.

2.3. Casa Lucio
Location: Calle de la Cava Baja, 35, Madrid 28005
A Madrid favorite, Casa Lucio is best known for its huevos rotos, but it also offers a wide range of traditional Spanish dishes. The rustic interior and authentic atmosphere make it a popular spot for locals, tourists, and even royals.

2.4. El Club Allard (2 Michelin Stars)
Location: Calle de Ferraz, 2, Madrid 28008
El Club Allard is known for its creative tasting menus that blend traditional Spanish ingredients with international influences. It offers an intimate and exclusive dining experience with beautifully crafted dishes.

2.5. StreetXO
Location: Calle de Serrano, 52, Madrid 28006
A more casual spin-off from DiverXO, StreetXO is where Chef Dabiz Muñoz combines Asian street food with Spanish flair. Expect bold flavors and an energetic, open-kitchen vibe.

2.6. La Barraca
Location: Calle de la Reina, 29, Madrid 28004

If you're craving authentic paella, La Barraca is the place to go. Specializing in rice dishes from Valencia, they offer a variety of paellas, including the traditional seafood paella and unique options like black rice with squid ink.

2.7. Mercado de San Miguel
Location: Plaza de San Miguel, s/n, Madrid 28005
While not a sit-down restaurant, Mercado de San Miguel is a must-visit food market for trying a wide range of Spanish delicacies, from jamón ibérico and oysters to freshly prepared tapas and artisan desserts. It's a lively spot to sample Madrid's culinary diversity.

From iconic dishes like cocido madrileño to Michelin-starred dining experiences, Madrid offers a culinary adventure that spans both tradition and innovation. Whether you're indulging in churros at San Ginés or experiencing the avant-garde creations at DiverXO, the city's diverse food scene is sure to satisfy every traveler's taste buds.

Food Markets and Street Food in Madrid

A Culinary Adventure

Madrid's food scene is a vibrant reflection of the city's rich history and cultural diversity. With bustling food markets offering gourmet delicacies and street vendors serving up authentic local snacks, exploring Madrid's culinary landscape is an experience that will delight every food lover. Whether you're in search of traditional Spanish dishes or looking to sample exotic street fare, Madrid's food markets and street corners are where the heart of its cuisine truly comes alive.

1. Madrid's Food Markets: Where Tradition Meets Innovation

In Madrid, food markets are not just places to buy groceries; they're hubs of community, culture, and culinary exploration. Here, you'll find a mix of old-world charm and modern gastronomy, perfect for tasting the city's best flavors in one lively space.

1.1. Mercado de San Miguel

Location: Plaza de San Miguel, s/n, Madrid 28005
Step into the iconic Mercado de San Miguel, and you'll be greeted by a feast for the senses. The market's historic iron-and-glass structure houses

some of Spain's finest gastronomic offerings. Imagine wandering through stalls of glistening seafood, artisanal cheeses, and gourmet tapas—each one more tempting than the last. For an elevated market experience, try an array of freshly shucked oysters paired with a crisp Spanish white wine or sample a variety of jamón ibérico, the prized ham of Spain.

Don't Miss:
- Pulpo a la Gallega (Galician-style octopus) with a side of patatas bravas.
- Sweet Treats: End your market tour with a gourmet selection of Spanish desserts, like turrón or churros dipped in rich chocolate.

1.2. Mercado de San Antón
Location: Calle de Augusto Figueroa, 24B, Madrid 28004

For those who want a trendy twist on traditional market fare, Mercado de San Antón in Chueca offers an exciting fusion of food and fashion. This chic, multi-level market features everything from traditional Spanish tapas to international cuisine, plus a rooftop terrace with panoramic views. Here, you can indulge in freshly made tostas (open-faced sandwiches) or sample Greek gyros and Peruvian ceviche, all while soaking in the lively atmosphere of one of Madrid's most fashionable neighborhoods.

Insider Tip: The rooftop bar is the perfect place for a sunset drink paired with tapas after a day of exploring the city.

1.3. Mercado de la Paz
Location: Calle de Ayala, 28, Madrid 28001
Nestled in the upscale Salamanca district, Mercado de la Paz is Madrid's hidden gem for foodies seeking an authentic market experience. Unlike the bustling San Miguel, this traditional market offers a more relaxed vibe. You'll find high-quality meats, seafood, and cheeses alongside charming stalls that serve fresh paella and croquetas. It's the perfect spot for those wanting to experience the city like a true Madrileño.

Try This: A plate of seafood paella paired with a glass of Ribera del Duero wine from one of the market's cozy stalls.

1.4. Mercado de Antón Martín
Location: Calle de Santa Isabel, 5, Madrid 28012
If you're an adventurous eater or a fan of global cuisine, Mercado de Antón Martín in the multicultural Lavapiés district is your go-to spot.

A melting pot of flavors, this market offers a diverse range of street food from around the world. You can grab Venezuelan arepas, Japanese sushi, or a piping hot bowl of traditional Spanish callos (tripe stew). It's a foodie paradise for those wanting to explore beyond the typical Spanish fare.

Don't Miss: Stop by one of the stalls offering fusion tapas, where Spanish ingredients meet international flair.

2. Street Food: A Taste of Madrid's Soul
In Madrid, street food isn't just fast—it's flavorful, iconic, and a true reflection of the city's culinary traditions. Whether you're taking a break between sightseeing or looking for a late-night snack, Madrid's street food offers quick bites that pack a punch of flavor.

2.1. Bocadillo de Calamares (Calamari Sandwich)
Crispy, golden rings of fried calamari stuffed into a fresh baguette—this is the bocadillo de calamares, one of Madrid's most beloved street foods. You'll often find locals munching on these sandwiches around Plaza Mayor, where some of the city's most famous calamari spots reside.
Where to Try It:

- La Campana (Calle de Botoneras, 6, Madrid 28012) – Just steps away from Plaza Mayor, this iconic spot serves some of the best calamari sandwiches in the city.
- El Brillante (Plaza del Emperador Carlos V, 8, Madrid 28012) – A go-to for locals near Atocha Station, this place is perfect for a quick, satisfying bite.

2.2. Churros con Chocolate

Madrid takes its churros seriously. These deep-fried dough pastries, dipped in a thick, velvety hot chocolate, are a must-try—whether as a morning treat or a late-night indulgence after a night out. A local favorite, churros con chocolate are the ultimate comfort food.

Where to Try It:
- Chocolatería San Ginés (Pasadizo de San Ginés, 5, Madrid 28013) – Serving churros since 1894, this iconic spot is open 24/7, making it the perfect post-party destination.

2.3. Croquetas

No Madrid street food journey is complete without a taste of croquetas. These creamy, bechamel-filled bites—often stuffed with ham, cod, or chicken—are crispy on the outside and melt-in-your-mouth delicious on the inside. You'll find croquetas on many tapas menus, but they're also a popular street food snack.

Where to Try It:
- Casa Labra (Calle de Tetuán, 12, Madrid 28013), Located near Puerta del Sol, this tavern is famous for its bacalao (cod) croquettes and has been serving them since 1860.

2.4. Tostas
A Madrid favorite, tostas are open-faced sandwiches topped with anything from jamón ibérico to smoked salmon. Easy to eat on the go, tostas are the perfect way to enjoy the flavors of Spain's finest ingredients in a single bite.

Where to Try It:
- Taberna La Daniela (Calle Cuchilleros, 9, Madrid 28005) This cozy tavern near La Latina is known for its delicious tostas with a wide variety of toppings.

3. Hidden Gems for Food Lovers

If you're the type of traveler who likes to venture off the beaten path, Madrid has plenty of hidden food gems that will satisfy your cravings for something different.

- ❖ Lavapiés District: Known for its multicultural vibe, Lavapiés offers a variety of international street food, from spicy Indian samosas to Venezuelan arepas. It's a neighborhood where food tells a global story, blending Spanish tradition with flavors from around the world.

- San Fernando Market: Located in the Lavapiés area, Mercado de San Fernando is a local favorite for fresh produce and artisanal food. You'll find everything from organic cheeses to craft beers, with plenty of street food stalls offering eclectic bites.

From the gourmet offerings at Mercado de San Miguel to the crispy delight of a calamari sandwich, Madrid's food markets and street vendors provide a window into the soul of the city. Whether you're seeking classic Spanish tapas or a fusion of international flavors, the markets and streets of Madrid promise a culinary adventure that will leave you hungry for more.

Shopping Districts and Souvenirs in Madrid

As you continue exploring Madrid, the city's unique shopping experience offers a perfect opportunity to immerse yourself in its local culture, fashion, and craftsmanship. In this chapter, we guide you through the various shopping districts, where each neighborhood has its own distinct character, ranging from high-end fashion streets to bustling traditional markets. Along the way, you'll discover some of the best souvenirs to bring home, each carrying a piece of Madrid's vibrant soul. This section will help you shop smart, ensuring you know exactly where to go and what to look for during your stay.

1. Madrid's Best Shopping Districts: Where Fashion Meets Tradition
Madrid's shopping districts are as varied as its neighborhoods, each offering a distinct shopping experience. Whether you're strolling through luxury boulevards or discovering hidden gems in charming alleys, there's something for everyone.

1.1. Gran Vía: Madrid's Broadway of Shopping

Location: Gran Vía, Madrid 28013

Madrid's Gran Vía is often compared to New York's Fifth Avenue or London's Oxford Street— a bustling boulevard lined with international fashion brands, flagship stores, and iconic department stores. If you're looking for big-name designers like Zara, H&M, and Primark, this is the place to go. The street also boasts beautiful architecture, making it a perfect mix of shopping and sightseeing.

What to Buy: International fashion brands, trendy clothing, accessories.

1.2. Salamanca District: Luxury and Designer Brands

Location: Calle de Serrano, Calle de Goya, Calle de Velázquez

For high-end shopping, look no further than Salamanca, Madrid's most upscale shopping district. Along Calle de Serrano and Calle de Goya, you'll find flagship stores for global luxury brands like Louis Vuitton, Gucci, and Chanel, as well as top Spanish designers like Adolfo Domínguez and Loewe. The area is also home to elegant boutiques offering everything from designer fashion to jewelry and fine leather goods.

What to Buy: Luxury fashion, designer accessories, high-end jewelry, and leather goods.

1.3. Fuencarral Street: The Bohemian Vibe
Location: Calle de Fuencarral, Madrid 28004
Calle de Fuencarral, located in the hip Malasaña and Chueca neighborhoods, is perfect for those looking for a more alternative, bohemian shopping experience. This pedestrian street is packed with independent boutiques, edgy clothing stores, and vintage shops. It's also a hub for urban and streetwear, making it a favorite for younger, fashion-forward shoppers.

What to Buy: Indie fashion, vintage clothing, streetwear, quirky accessories.

1.4. El Rastro: Madrid's Famous Flea Market
Location: Plaza de Cascorro and Ribera de Curtidores, La Latina, Madrid 28005
For a completely different shopping experience, El Rastro is Madrid's largest and most famous flea market, held every Sunday in the La Latina neighborhood. The market sprawls through the streets, offering everything from antique furniture and vintage clothing to handmade crafts and quirky souvenirs. It's a great place to find

one-of-a-kind items, and the atmosphere alone makes it a must-visit.

What to Buy: Antiques, handmade crafts, vintage finds, quirky souvenirs.

1.5. Mercado de San Miguel and Mercado de San Antón: Gourmet Souvenirs
Locations: Plaza de San Miguel, s/n (Mercado de San Miguel) | Calle de Augusto Figueroa, 24B (Mercado de San Antón)
If you prefer edible souvenirs, Madrid's gourmet food markets are ideal. At Mercado de San Miguel and Mercado de San Antón, you can pick up some of Spain's finest foods, including jamón ibérico (Iberian ham), queso manchego (Manchego cheese), olive oil, and gourmet chocolates. These markets offer high-quality, locally sourced products that are perfect for taking a taste of Spain back home.

What to Buy: Gourmet food items, Iberian ham, Manchego cheese, olive oil, Spanish wines.

2. Unique Souvenirs from Madrid: Bringing Home a Piece of Spain
Madrid is full of unique treasures, from traditional Spanish crafts to locally produced goods. Here are

some must-have souvenirs that will remind you of your trip.

2.1. Jamón Ibérico (Iberian Ham)

One of the most iconic Spanish products, jamón ibérico is a prized delicacy made from acorn-fed Iberian pigs. This cured ham is rich in flavor and makes for a luxurious gift to bring back from Madrid. You can find vacuum-sealed packs in gourmet markets like Mercado de San Miguel or specialized ham shops such as Museo del Jamón.

Where to Buy: Museo del Jamón (Calle Mayor, 7), Mercado de San Miguel, gourmet food stores.

2.2. Ceramics and Pottery

Spain is renowned for its beautifully hand-painted ceramics, and Madrid is a great place to find them. Look for colorful talavera pottery, plates, bowls, and tiles with traditional Spanish motifs. These make wonderful decorative pieces and can be found in markets like El Rastro or specialty ceramic shops.

Where to Buy: El Rastro, Cerámica Santa Ana (Calle de las Maravillas, 3, 28015 Madrid).

2.3. Flamenco Accessories

Madrid is one of the best places to buy flamenco-themed souvenirs. From hand-painted abanicos (fans) to castañuelas (castanets) and vibrant flamenco dresses, these items are perfect mementos of Spain's passionate dance culture. You'll find authentic flamenco accessories in shops around Plaza Mayor and El Rastro.

Where to Buy: Souvenir shops near Plaza Mayor, flamenco boutiques in La Latina.

2.4. Espadrilles (Alpargatas)

Espadrilles, known as alpargatas in Spanish, are traditional canvas shoes with woven jute soles. These shoes are comfortable, stylish, and a quintessential part of Spanish fashion. Madrid has several stores that sell hand-made, high-quality espadrilles in various colors and patterns.

Where to Buy: Casa Hernanz (Calle de Toledo, 18, Madrid 28005) – A family-run shop that has been making espadrilles since 1840.

2.5. Spanish Leather Goods

Spain is famous for its high-quality leather goods, including handbags, belts, and wallets. Madrid's shopping districts, particularly Salamanca, offer a range of leather products, from luxury brands to artisanal shops. Look for handcrafted pieces that will last a lifetime.

Where to Buy: Calle de Serrano (for luxury brands), El Rastro (for handmade items).

2.6. Spanish Wine and Olive Oil

Spain is one of the world's top wine producers, and bringing back a bottle of Rioja or Ribera del Duero wine is a great way to remember your trip. Spanish olive oil is also a prized product, known for its high quality and rich flavor. You can buy beautifully packaged bottles of olive oil and wine from gourmet shops and markets around the city.

Where to Buy: Mercado de San Miguel, Club del Gourmet at El Corte Inglés.

3. Tips for Shopping in Madrid

- Shop Tax-Free: If you're visiting from outside the EU, don't forget to claim your tax refund on purchases over a certain amount. Many shops participate in Tax-Free Shopping, so ask for your receipt and fill out the necessary forms at the airport.

- Bargaining: In markets like El Rastro, bargaining is common and can add a fun element to your shopping experience. Don't be afraid to haggle a bit to get the best price.
- Best Times to Shop: The best time to shop is during Madrid's seasonal sales, known as rebajas, in January and July. You'll find deep discounts on fashion and other goods.

From the luxury boutiques of Salamanca to the quirky treasures at El Rastro and gourmet delights from Madrid's food markets, shopping in Madrid offers something for everyone. Whether you're picking up a bottle of Spanish olive oil, a hand-painted ceramic tile, or a pair of traditional espadrilles, Madrid's shopping districts are the perfect place to find memorable souvenirs that capture the essence of this vibrant city.

CHAPTER FIVE

DAY TRIPS AND HIDDEN GEMS

Best Day Trips from Madrid: Exploring Toledo, Segovia, El Escorial, and More

While Madrid itself offers an abundance of attractions, the surrounding region is rich with history, culture, and stunning landscapes that make for incredible day trips. Just a short journey from the bustling capital, you can find ancient cities, medieval castles, and UNESCO World Heritage sites, each offering its own unique charm. This chapter highlights the best day trips from Madrid, including Toledo, Segovia, El Escorial, and other nearby gems, allowing you to experience more of Spain's diverse history and architecture.

1. Toledo: The City of Three Cultures

Distance from Madrid: 70 km (43 miles) | Travel **Time:** 30 minutes by train

Known as the City of Three Cultures due to its rich blend of Christian, Muslim, and Jewish heritage, Toledo is one of the most popular day trips from Madrid. The entire city is a UNESCO World Heritage Site, offering visitors a step back in time with its winding medieval streets, towering cathedrals, and historic synagogues.

Top Attractions:
- Toledo Cathedral: A stunning Gothic masterpiece, regarded as one of the most beautiful cathedrals in Spain.
- Alcázar of Toledo: A massive stone fortress perched atop a hill, offering panoramic views of the city and surrounding landscape.
- El Greco Museum: Dedicated to the famous painter El Greco, this museum showcases some of his finest works.
- Monastery of San Juan de los Reyes: A beautiful example of Gothic architecture with elaborate cloisters.

Must-Do: Walk along the ancient Puente de San Martín bridge for breathtaking views of Toledo's old town, especially at sunset.

2. Segovia: Roman Aqueducts and Fairytale Castles

Distance from Madrid: 90 km (56 miles) | **Travel Time:** 1 hour by train

Segovia is famous for its awe-inspiring Roman aqueduct, fairytale-like Alcázar, and charming historic streets. With a mix of Roman and medieval architecture, Segovia transports visitors to a different era, making it a magical destination just outside Madrid.

Top Attractions:
- Roman Aqueduct: Built in the 1st century AD, this massive aqueduct is a marvel of Roman engineering, stretching across the city's skyline.
- Alcázar of Segovia: A fairytale castle perched atop a hill, said to have inspired Disney's Cinderella Castle.
- Segovia Cathedral: Known as the "Lady of Cathedrals," this late Gothic cathedral dominates the city's main square.

Must-Do: Climb to the top of the Alcázar for stunning views of the surrounding countryside and mountains.

3. El Escorial: A Royal Monastery and Spanish History

Distance from Madrid: 50 km (31 miles) | Travel Time: 45 minutes by train

The Royal Monastery of El Escorial is one of Spain's most important historical and architectural landmarks. Built in the 16th century under the reign of King Philip II, this vast complex served as a royal palace, monastery, and mausoleum for Spanish royalty. It is also a UNESCO World Heritage Site.

Top Attractions:
- The Basilica: Featuring impressive religious artwork and intricate architecture.
- The Royal Pantheon: The resting place of Spanish monarchs, located in the depths of the complex.
- The Library of El Escorial: A beautiful Renaissance library with thousands of ancient manuscripts.
- The Gardens: The neatly manicured gardens offer a peaceful retreat with views of the surrounding mountains.

Must-Do: Explore the stunning Hall of Battles, which features large frescoes depicting significant battles in Spanish history.

4. Ávila: The Walled City

Distance from Madrid: 110 km (68 miles) | Travel Time: 1 hour 30 minutes by train

Famed for its remarkably well-preserved medieval walls, Ávila is another UNESCO World Heritage Site that is perfect for a day trip. Its majestic walls, which date back to the 11th century, encircle the city and provide a dramatic backdrop to the narrow streets and historic churches within.

Top Attractions:
- Ávila Walls: Walk along the top of these impressive medieval fortifications for panoramic views of the city and countryside.
- Ávila Cathedral: Known as the first Gothic cathedral in Spain, it is integrated into the city walls and showcases both Romanesque and Gothic elements.
- Convent of Saint Teresa: Dedicated to Saint Teresa of Ávila, a significant figure in Spanish religious history.

Must-Do: Stroll through the old town and enjoy a meal of chuletón de Ávila, a famous local steak, in one of the traditional restaurants.

5. Aranjuez: Royal Gardens and Palaces
Distance from Madrid: 50 km (31 miles) | Travel Time: 45 minutes by train
Known for its sprawling royal gardens and magnificent palace, Aranjuez is a peaceful escape from the hustle and bustle of Madrid. The Royal Palace of Aranjuez served as a spring residence for Spanish monarchs, and its surrounding gardens are perfect for a relaxing afternoon stroll.

Top Attractions:
- Royal Palace of Aranjuez: A stunning palace with lavish interiors and impressive collections of art and historical artifacts.
- The Gardens of Aranjuez: These expansive gardens, including the Jardín del Príncipe and Jardín de la Isla, are filled with fountains, statues, and walking paths.
- Museo de las Falúas Reales: This museum houses the royal barges used by Spanish kings and queens to navigate the Tagus River.

Must-Do: Take a leisurely boat ride along the Tagus River or enjoy a traditional fresas de Aranjuez (local strawberries) in season.

6. Chinchón: A Traditional Spanish Village
Distance from Madrid: 45 km (28 miles) | Travel Time: 1 hour by bus

If you're looking for a more off-the-beaten-path experience, Chinchón is a charming village known for its medieval Plaza Mayor, traditional festivals, and local wines. The town's quiet, rustic charm offers a peaceful contrast to Madrid's bustling energy.

Top Attractions:
- Plaza Mayor: A picturesque square that turns into a bullring during festivals. The surrounding buildings feature traditional wooden balconies.
- Castle of Chinchón: A 15th-century fortress located on a hill overlooking the town.
- Chinchón Wine: Visit local wineries to sample the region's signature wines, especially anís, a local liqueur.

Must-Do: Visit during one of the town's festivals, such as Semana Santa or the Grape Harvest Festival, to experience Chinchón's vibrant local traditions.

Whether you're marveling at the Roman aqueduct in Segovia, walking through Toledo's medieval streets, or relaxing in the royal gardens of Aranjuez, these day trips from Madrid offer an unforgettable glimpse into Spain's history, culture, and natural beauty. With so many remarkable destinations just a short ride away, these excursions make for the perfect addition to your Madrid itinerary.

Off the Beaten Path: Hidden Neighborhoods and Unique Experiences

Beyond the iconic landmarks and bustling tourist spots, Madrid is a city brimming with hidden gems and lesser-known neighborhoods that offer an authentic glimpse into its local life. Venturing off the beaten path will lead you to charming streets, quirky districts, and unique experiences that capture the true essence of the city. This chapter will guide you through Madrid's hidden neighborhoods and provide insider tips on experiencing the city like a local.

1. La Latina: A Neighborhood Steeped in Tradition

Location: South of Plaza Mayor

La Latina is one of Madrid's most charming and traditional neighborhoods, characterized by its narrow, winding streets, historic architecture, and vibrant tapas bars. This area is often overlooked by tourists but offers an authentic Madrid experience with its lively atmosphere and rich cultural heritage.

Top Experiences:
- Cava Baja Street: Known for its abundance of tapas bars and eateries, this street is

perfect for sampling local delicacies and experiencing Madrid's culinary scene.
- El Rastro Flea Market: Held every Sunday, this sprawling market offers everything from antiques and vintage clothing to unique souvenirs and street food.
- Church of San Andrés: A lesser-known historical gem with a beautiful baroque façade and serene interior.

Must-Do: Wander through the Plaza de la Cebada and enjoy the local markets and street performers. The area also hosts various festivals throughout the year, providing a lively and colorful atmosphere.

2. Malasaña: The Hipster Hub
Location: North of Gran Vía
Malasaña is Madrid's bohemian and trendy district, known for its alternative vibe, vintage shops, and vibrant street art. This neighborhood is a haven for creatives and young locals, offering a glimpse into Madrid's modern, eclectic side.

Top Experiences:
- Tribal Area: Explore this area for quirky shops, unique cafes, and street art. It's a

hotspot for vintage lovers and independent designers.
- Plaza del 2 de Mayo: The heart of Malasaña, where you can find lively bars, boutique shops, and frequent cultural events.
- Street Art: Take a walking tour to admire the impressive street art and murals that adorn the walls of the neighborhood.

Must-Do: Visit one of the many trendy coffee shops or bars, such as Toma Café or La Vía Láctea, and soak in the neighborhood's laid-back, creative atmosphere.

3. Chueca: The Vibrant LGBTQ+ District
- Location: Adjacent to Malasaña

Chueca is Madrid's LGBTQ+ friendly neighborhood, celebrated for its open-minded and inclusive culture. Known for its lively nightlife, colorful festivals, and eclectic shops, Chueca offers a vibrant and welcoming experience for all visitors.

Top Experiences:
- Plaza de Chueca: The main square of the neighborhood, surrounded by cafes, bars, and shops. It's the perfect place to start exploring.

- Mercado de San Antón: A modern food market where you can sample gourmet foods, fresh produce, and local specialties.
- FestiMAD: If visiting in May, enjoy the annual alternative music festival that takes place in various venues throughout the neighborhood.

Must-Do: Explore the diverse array of bars and clubs along Calle de Fuencarral and Calle de Hortaleza, which come alive at night with music and dance.

4. Lavapiés: A Multicultural Melting Pot
- **Location: Southeast of Gran Vía**

Lavapiés is known for its multicultural vibe and artistic community. This neighborhood reflects Madrid's diverse population, with influences from around the world evident in its restaurants, shops, and cultural institutions.

Top Experiences:
- Ronda de Atocha: A street lined with international eateries and shops, offering a global dining experience.
- Tabacalera: A cultural center housed in a former tobacco factory, featuring

exhibitions, workshops, and community events.
- La Casa Encendida: A cultural space known for its contemporary art exhibitions, music performances, and social initiatives.

Must-Do: Visit the Plaza de Lavapiés and enjoy the lively street performances, or explore the neighborhood's diverse culinary offerings, from Ethiopian to Indian cuisine.

5. Chamberí: The Underrated Gem
- Location: North of the city center

Chamberí is a residential area that offers a quieter, more authentic Madrid experience. Known for its charming streets, beautiful architecture, and local markets, Chamberí is often overlooked by tourists but is worth exploring for a taste of traditional Madrid life.

Top Experiences:
- Andén 0: A preserved section of the old Chamberí metro station, offering a fascinating glimpse into Madrid's transportation history.
- Plaza de Chamberí: A picturesque square surrounded by historic buildings, cafes, and local shops.

- Chamberí Market: A lively local market where you can sample fresh produce and traditional Spanish foods.

Must-Do: Enjoy a leisurely stroll through the Parque de Chamberí and visit one of the neighborhood's traditional taverns for a relaxing meal.

6. Conde Duque: The Cultural Enclave
- Location: West of the city center

Conde Duque is an emerging cultural hotspot in Madrid, known for its historic buildings, cultural centers, and artistic events. The neighborhood is home to a range of cultural institutions and offers a glimpse into Madrid's evolving artistic scene.

Top Experiences:
- Centro Cultural Conde Duque: A former barracks turned cultural center, hosting art exhibitions, concerts, and theater performances.
- Plaza de Conde Duque: A spacious square with a relaxed atmosphere, perfect for a leisurely afternoon.
- Café del Conde: A charming café known for its local atmosphere and great coffee.

Must-Do: Attend a cultural event or exhibition at the Centro Cultural Conde Duque and explore the surrounding streets for a taste of Madrid's creative side.

Exploring these off-the-beaten-path neighborhoods will provide you with a deeper understanding of Madrid's diverse character and hidden charm. Whether you're soaking in the bohemian vibes of Malasaña, savoring international cuisine in Lavapiés, or wandering through the quiet streets of Chamberí, these unique experiences offer a refreshing contrast to the city's more tourist-centric attractions.

Family-Friendly Activities and Attractions in Madrid

Families visiting Madrid will find a wide array of exciting activities and attractions that cater to children and adults alike. Whether it's exploring lush parks, engaging with wildlife, or delving into the city's history through interactive museums, Madrid offers numerous opportunities for family-friendly fun. This guide provides a closer look at the best spots to enjoy with kids, ensuring everyone has a memorable experience.

1. Parque del Retiro: Madrid Green Oasis

- Location: City Center

Parque del Retiro is a vast green space in the heart of Madrid, offering a perfect escape for families. With wide open spaces for picnicking, playgrounds, and beautiful walking paths, it's a place where children can burn off energy while parents relax.

Top Attractions:
- Rowboat Rides on the Retiro Lake: Rent a boat and paddle across the serene lake, offering fun for both kids and adults.

- The Crystal Palace: A beautiful glass building that hosts free art exhibitions and is surrounded by picturesque gardens.
- Playgrounds and Puppet Shows: Several playgrounds are scattered throughout the park, and on weekends, there are often puppet shows for children.

Must-Do: Visit the La Rosaleda (Rose Garden) and the Parque de Atracciones, a nearby amusement park with rides for kids of all ages.

2. Madrid Zoo and Aquarium: A Day of Wildlife Adventure

- Location: Casa de Campo Park

Located in the expansive Casa de Campo Park, the Madrid Zoo and Aquarium is one of the largest and most popular family-friendly attractions in the city. It houses a wide variety of animals from around the world, as well as marine exhibits in its aquarium.

Top Attractions:
- Panda House: Madrid Zoo is one of the few zoos in the world that houses giant pandas, a must-see for kids.
- Dolphin Shows: Enjoy captivating dolphin performances in the zoo's large aquarium.
- Animal Encounters: Meet animals up close, including birds of prey, reptiles, and small mammals.

Must-Do: Take a ride on the zoo's train to tour the entire facility while getting a close-up view of many of the animal exhibits.

3. The Royal Palace: A Majestic Tour
Location: City Center
The Royal Palace of Madrid is an awe-inspiring architectural gem that offers a glimpse into the history and splendor of Spain's monarchy. While children will marvel at the grandiose rooms and lavish decor, the palace also offers engaging tours designed for families.

Top Attractions:
- Guided Family Tours: These tours are tailored to children, providing fun facts and interactive elements to keep younger visitors entertained.
- The Royal Armory: Showcasing a collection of medieval armor, swords, and weapons, which is often a favorite for kids.
- Palace Gardens: The expansive gardens are perfect for a relaxing stroll or a family picnic after your visit.

Must-Do: Be sure to catch the Changing of the Guard ceremony, which occurs every Wednesday and Saturday outside the palace.

4. Faunia: An Immersive Wildlife Park
- Location: Vicálvaro

Faunia is a unique wildlife park that combines elements of a zoo and a botanical garden, offering families the chance to explore different ecosystems from around the world. With interactive exhibits and hands-on experiences, Faunia is an engaging way for kids to learn about animals and nature.

Top Attractions:
- Ecosystems: Explore different habitats, including the Amazon Jungle, Antarctica,

and the African Savannah, each home to a variety of animals.
- interactive Experiences: Kids can feed the animals, meet penguins, and interact with farm animals at the Little Farm exhibit.
- Dinosaur Exhibit: A thrilling attraction where children can learn about prehistoric creatures and see life-size dinosaur models.

Must-Do: Participate in a Penguin Encounter, where families can get up close to these adorable creatures in the park's Antarctic zone.

5. Museo de Cera: Madrid's Wax Museum

- Location: Paseo de Recoletos

For a fun and educational experience, families can visit the Museo de Cera, Madrid's wax museum, where children can see lifelike figures of historical figures, celebrities, and fictional characters. This museum brings history and pop culture to life in a way that appeals to both kids and adults.

Top Attractions:
- Historical Figures: Meet wax figures of famous personalities like Christopher Columbus, Cervantes, and Queen Isabella I.
- Star Wars and Superheroes: Kids will love seeing their favorite characters from popular movies and TV shows.
- The Terror Train: A fun ride through a spooky underground tunnel filled with surprises.

Must-Do: Don't miss the Interactive Space section, where children can engage in multimedia exhibits and learn about science in an entertaining way.

6. Teleférico: A Bird's-Eye View of Madrid
Location: Casa de Campo Park

For an exciting and scenic adventure, take a ride on Madrid's Teleférico, a cable car that offers breathtaking aerial views of the city. The ride takes you from the Rosales area to Casa de Campo, passing over the Manzanares River and offering stunning views of Madrid's skyline and famous landmarks.

Top Attractions:
- Scenic Views: Get panoramic views of Parque del Oeste, Madrid Rio, and the Royal Palace from the cable car.
- Casa de Campo: Once you reach the end of the ride, explore Casa de Campo, which offers playgrounds, hiking trails, and picnic areas.
- Family-Friendly Cafes: Enjoy a snack or meal at the park's cafes while taking in the picturesque scenery.

Must-Do: Take binoculars to spot some of Madrid's landmarks from above, and enjoy a family picnic in the peaceful surroundings of Casa de Campo.

7. Museo del Ferrocarril: A Journey Through Railway History

Location: Delicias

The Museo del Ferrocarril (Railway Museum) is a fascinating destination for children who love trains. Housed in a historic train station, the museum features vintage locomotives, carriages, and interactive exhibits that showcase the history of Spain's railways.

Top Attractions:
- Old Locomotives: Explore a collection of restored steam engines, diesel trains, and electric trains from different eras.

- Train Rides: On select weekends, the museum offers short train rides on historical carriages.
- Interactive Exhibits: Children can explore the inside of trains and learn how railways have evolved over time.

Must-Do: Visit on a weekend to ride the Little Train, an outdoor miniature railway that's perfect for younger children.

8. Madrid Rio Park: Outdoor Fun for the Whole Family

Location: Along the Manzanares River

Madrid Rio is a sprawling park that stretches along the Manzanares River and offers a wide range of outdoor activities for families. From playgrounds and water fountains to bike paths and scenic walks, Madrid Rio provides the perfect setting for an active day out with the family.

Top Attractions:
- Water Play Areas: In the warmer months, kids can cool off in the park's water fountains and splash areas.
- Playgrounds: The park boasts some of the most impressive playgrounds in the city, with climbing structures, swings, and slides for all ages.
- Bike and Scooter Paths: Rent bikes or scooters and explore the park along its dedicated paths.

Must-Do: Don't miss the Arganzuela Footbridge, a striking architectural feature of the park, and pack a picnic to enjoy by the river.

CHAPTER SIX
Practical Information And Resources

Health, Safety, and Accessibility
When traveling to Madrid, it's important to be prepared with practical information on health, safety, and accessibility. Whether you're a solo traveler, a family, or a person with specific mobility needs, Madrid provides a range of resources and infrastructure to ensure a smooth and enjoyable visit. Here's what to keep in mind to make your trip safe and comfortable.

1. Health Services: Staying Well While Traveling
Madrid offers excellent healthcare services, with both public and private hospitals and clinics that are easily accessible to tourists. Pharmacies are widespread, with many open 24/7, offering over-the-counter medications and advice.

- ❖ Emergency Medical Services: In case of a medical emergency, call 112 for immediate assistance. Public hospitals such as Hospital Universitario La Paz and Hospital Universitario Clínico San Carlos are well-equipped and staffed with English-speaking professionals.

- ❖ Travel Insurance: While Spain's healthcare system is top-tier, it's advisable to have travel insurance that covers medical expenses, especially if you're using private hospitals or clinics. EU citizens should carry their European Health Insurance Card (EHIC) for access to state-provided healthcare.

- ❖ Pharmacies: Look for the green cross sign, which indicates a pharmacy (farmacia). Many provide basic healthcare services, and some are open 24 hours, such as Farmacia Central on Gran Vía.

2. Safety in Madrid: Keeping Your Trip Stress-Free

Madrid is generally a safe city, but as with any large urban area, it's important to remain vigilant, especially in crowded tourist spots. Petty theft, such as pickpocketing, can occur in busy areas, but serious crime is rare.

- ❖ Pickpocketing Prevention: Popular spots like Puerta del Sol, Plaza Mayor, and Gran

Vía attract large crowds. Be mindful of your belongings, especially in these areas. Keep valuables close, avoid carrying large amounts of cash, and use anti-theft bags if possible.

- ❖ Police Presence: Madrid has a visible police presence, particularly in tourist-heavy areas. The National Police and Municipal Police are approachable, and they can assist in English if needed. For non-emergency assistance, you can call the local police at 091.

- ❖ Nighttime Safety: While Madrid's nightlife is famous, it's best to avoid walking alone late at night in unfamiliar areas. Stick to well-lit streets, and use reputable transportation services like Uber, Cabify, or licensed taxis.

3. Accessibility: Navigating Madrid with Ease

Madrid is becoming increasingly accessible for travelers with disabilities, offering a variety of services and accommodations to ensure everyone can enjoy the city.

- Public Transportation: The Madrid Metro system is wheelchair accessible, with over 70% of stations equipped with elevators and ramps. Additionally, EMT Madrid buses are all accessible, with low floors and designated spaces for wheelchairs. The Cercanías suburban trains also have accessible carriages.

- Accessible Tourist Attractions: Many of Madrid's top attractions, including the Royal Palace, Museo del Prado, and Reina Sofía Museum, offer accessibility features such as ramps, elevators, and adapted restrooms. The Parque del Retiro has wide, smooth paths for easy wheelchair navigation.

- Hotels and Accommodations: Many hotels across Madrid provide accessible rooms and facilities for guests with mobility issues. It's advisable to check the hotel's accessibility options in advance and make specific requests if needed.

Budgeting Tips and Free Things to Do

Exploring Madrid doesn't have to break the bank. The city offers numerous budget-friendly activities, along with plenty of free attractions, making it easy to enjoy the culture, history, and lifestyle without spending a fortune. Here are some practical budgeting tips and highlights of free experiences you can enjoy while visiting Madrid.

1. Budgeting Tips: Maximizing Your Money in Madrid

- ❖ Accommodation: Look for budget-friendly accommodation in central locations such as Lavapiés or Malasaña. Hostels, guesthouses, and vacation rentals often offer excellent rates compared to high-end hotels. Booking in advance or during the off-season (winter, except Christmas) can significantly lower costs.

- ❖ Public Transportation: Purchase the Madrid Tourist Travel Pass (Abono Turístico) for unlimited travel on the metro, buses, and suburban trains within the city. It's available for 1 to 7 days and offers substantial savings compared to single tickets. Alternatively, walk as much as possible—Madrid's central districts are easy to explore on foot.

- ❖ Eating Out: Avoid tourist-heavy restaurants around Puerta del Sol or Gran Vía, where prices are higher. Instead, opt for menú del día (daily set menus) at local restaurants, which offer two or three courses, bread, and a drink for a fixed price—typically between €10 and €15. You'll also find affordable tapas bars in neighborhoods like La Latina and Chueca.

- ❖ Grocery Stores and Markets: For budget-conscious travelers, shopping at local markets like Mercado de San Fernando or grocery stores can save money on meals. Many markets also have affordable food stalls where you can enjoy local cuisine for a fraction of restaurant prices.

- ❖ Free Walking Tours: Several companies offer free walking tours of Madrid, providing a great way to learn about the city's history and culture without the cost of a guided tour. While these tours are technically free, it's customary to tip the guide at the end based on your satisfaction.

2. Free Things to Do in Madrid

Madrid offers a surprising number of free attractions, from stunning museums with free entry times to historic landmarks and scenic parks. Here are some of the top free experiences to enjoy:

A. Explore Madrid's Iconic Parks
- Retiro Park: One of Madrid's most famous parks, Parque del Retiro is free to enter and perfect for a leisurely day out. You can stroll through its beautiful gardens, admire the Crystal Palace, or relax by the lake.

- Madrid Río: A modern green space along the Manzanares River, Madrid Río is ideal for walking, cycling, or having a picnic while enjoying views of the city. It features playgrounds, fountains, and cultural events.

- Temple of Debod: A unique ancient Egyptian temple located in Parque del Oeste, the Temple of Debod offers stunning views of the sunset over the city. Entry is free, and you can explore both the temple and the surrounding gardens.

B. Free Museum Days and Cultural Experiences

- Museo del Prado: One of the world's most renowned art museums, the Prado Museum offers free entry every evening (6–8 pm Monday to Saturday and 5–7 pm on Sundays and holidays). Explore masterpieces by Velázquez, Goya, and El Greco without paying a cent.

- Reina Sofía Museum: Home to Picasso's Guernica and other modern masterpieces, the Reina Sofía offers free entry on Monday, Wednesday to Saturday from 7–9 pm, and on Sundays from 12:30 pm to 2:30 pm. This is a fantastic opportunity to see Spain's most famous contemporary art collection.

- Museo Thyssen-Bornemisza: Known for its diverse collection of European art, the Thyssen Museum allows free entry on Mondays from 12–4 pm. This is a great chance to explore works by artists from the Renaissance to the 20th century.

- Palacio Real Gardens: While the Royal Palace requires an entry fee, the palace's stunning gardens, Jardines de Sabatini, and Campo del Moro, are free to visit. You can walk through these manicured spaces, take in the grand views, and capture beautiful photos.

3. **Historic and Architectural Sight**
   - Puerta del Sol and Plaza Mayor: These central squares are iconic spots to explore for free. Wander through Puerta del Sol, known for its famous Tío Pepe sign and the Kilometer Zero marker, or relax in Plaza Mayor, a grand square surrounded by beautiful architecture and lively street performers.

   - Gran Vía: Stroll down Madrid's most famous shopping street, Gran Vía, and take in its impressive early 20th-century architecture. This bustling avenue is lined with theaters, shops, and historic buildings, offering a great window-shopping experience.

   - Catedral de la Almudena: Located next to the Royal Palace, the Almudena Cathedral is free to enter and explore. This modern cathedral blends neo-Gothic and contemporary elements, offering stunning views from its dome (although there's a fee for the rooftop).

4. Cultural and Community Events

- ❖ Madrid's Festivals: Many of Madrid's famous festivals, such as San Isidro in May and La Paloma in August, offer free concerts, parades, and cultural performances in the streets. These lively celebrations are a fantastic way to experience local traditions without spending any money.

- ❖ Street Performances: In busy areas like Plaza Mayor and Puerta del Sol, you'll often find street performers—musicians, dancers, and even live statues—offering free entertainment. It's a lively part of Madrid's culture that adds vibrancy to the city's daily life.

Maps, Suggested Itineraries, and Useful Apps

Planning your journey through Madrid is essential to making the most of your time in the city. Whether you're here for a day, a weekend, or a week, this section provides suggested itineraries, helpful maps, and the best apps to enhance your travel experience. These tools will help you navigate the city with ease and explore Madrid's rich culture, history, and modern attractions.

1. Maps: Navigating Madrid Like a Local
- ❖ Madrid City Map: Downloadable maps, such as those provided by the Madrid Tourism Board, offer detailed views of key areas, including the historical center, public transportation routes, and main attractions. Hard copies of these maps are available at tourist information centers throughout the city.

- ❖ Metro and Bus Maps: Madrid's metro system is extensive and easy to navigate. The Metro de Madrid app provides a full map of the metro and suburban train lines, while physical maps are posted in every station. Similarly, bus routes are well-marked on EMT Madrid maps, which cover the entire city and suburbs.

❖ Neighborhood Maps: Major neighborhoods like Malasaña, Chueca, Lavapiés, and Salamanca each have their own charm. A walking map of these areas can help you discover hidden gems like boutique shops, cafes, street art, and historical landmarks.

2. Suggested Itineraries: Tailored to Your Time in Madrid

Depending on how much time you have in the city, these itineraries will guide you through must-see spots, ensuring a rich experience whether you're in Madrid for a day or a week.

One-Day Itinerary: Madrid in a Day
- ❖ Morning:
- Start with a visit to the Royal Palace and Plaza de Oriente.
- Walk through the nearby Almudena Cathedral and enjoy the architecture.

- ❖ Midday: Head to Plaza Mayor for a light lunch at one of the outdoor terraces or sample tapas at Mercado de San Miguel.

- ❖ Afternoon:
- Visit the Museo del Prado to see its world-famous art collection.
- Stroll through Parque del Retiro, taking time to see the Crystal Palace and the central lake.

- ❖ Evening: Finish the day with dinner in the lively La Latina neighborhood, sampling traditional Spanish tapas and wine.

Weekend Itinerary: A 2-3 Day Exploration
- ❖ Day 1: Follow the one-day itinerary above to cover the key highlights.

- ❖ Day 2:
- Begin with a visit to the Reina Sofía Museum to see Picasso's Guernica and other modern art.
- Walk down Gran Vía, taking in the architecture and exploring some of the high-end shops.
- Enjoy a leisurely lunch in the trendy Malasaña neighborhood.

- Spend the afternoon at El Rastro, Madrid's famous flea market (Sundays only), or visit Templo de Debod for a sunset view over the city.

- Day 3: Take a short day trip to Toledo or Segovia, or explore the hidden streets and lesser-known attractions in Lavapiés or Chueca.

Week-Long Itinerary: Dive Deep into Madrid

- Days 1-3: Follow the two-day itinerary to explore the major sites in Madrid's center.

- Day 4:
  - Visit El Escorial or Aranjuez, two beautiful historical towns just outside Madrid.
  - Return to the city and spend the evening in Salamanca, Madrid's upscale shopping and dining district.

- Day 5: Explore Madrid's green spaces:
  - Spend the morning in Casa de Campo, with the option to visit the Madrid Zoo or take a cable car ride for panoramic views.

- Later, visit Parque del Capricho, a hidden gem offering beautiful, tranquil gardens away from the crowds.

❖ Day 6: Focus on Madrid's vibrant art and culture scene with visits to smaller galleries, such as CaixaForum and Matadero Madrid, a contemporary art center in a former slaughterhouse.

❖ Day 7: Enjoy a free day to revisit your favorite spots or take a final day trip to nearby Ávila or Cuenca.

3. Useful Apps: Enhancing Your Madrid Experience

Several apps can make your visit to Madrid smoother and more enjoyable by providing real-time information, helping you navigate, or offering insights into the city's attractions.

❖ Metro de Madrid: This official app provides detailed maps of the metro system, real-time train schedules, and route planners. It's essential for navigating the city's public transportation efficiently.

- EMT Madrid: If you plan to take buses, this app offers real-time updates on bus schedules, route maps, and stop locations. It's particularly helpful for routes that don't follow the metro lines.

- Google Maps: Of course, Google Maps is indispensable for walking directions and public transport guidance. It's especially helpful for locating restaurants, cafes, and attractions while exploring the city.

- GuruWalk: If you're interested in free walking tours, GuruWalk connects you with local guides offering tours based on tips. It's a great way to discover the city's hidden gems from a local perspective.

- The Fork (ElTenedor): This app allows you to browse restaurant reviews, make reservations, and access discounts at some of Madrid's best eateries. Perfect for finding a budget-friendly meal or a top dining spot.

- Prado Guide: The Prado Museum has an official app that serves as a digital guide to the museum's collection. It offers audio tours, detailed information about the artworks, and suggested itineraries for your visit.

- ❖ Madrid Móvil: The Madrid Móvil app is perfect for general city information, including updates on local events, transportation schedules, and public services. It's useful for finding out about festivals or local happenings during your visit.

- ❖ Cabify and Uber: Both Cabify and Uber operate in Madrid and are excellent alternatives to traditional taxis, especially for late-night rides or trips to areas not easily accessible by public transport.

With these maps, itineraries, and apps in hand, navigating Madrid becomes simple and efficient, allowing you to focus on enjoying all that this magnificent city has to offer. Whether you're discovering iconic landmarks, hidden gems, or enjoying local culture, you'll be well-prepared to explore the city with confidence.

Conclusion

Madrid is more than just a destination; it's a vibrant, living tapestry woven with history, culture, art, and unforgettable experiences. From the grand elegance of Plaza Mayor to the artistic wonders housed in the Museo del Prado, the city offers an irresistible blend of old-world charm and modern energy that speaks to every type of traveler.

Over the course of this guide, we've journeyed through Madrid's iconic landmarks, explored its hidden neighborhoods, and sampled the best of its world-renowned cuisine. Whether you're captivated by the majesty of the Royal Palace, enchanted by the soulful rhythms of flamenco, or simply enjoying an afternoon wandering the lush Parque del Retiro, Madrid's diverse offerings cater to every whim and interest.

Beyond its sights, what truly sets Madrid apart is its spirit, the warmth of its people, the liveliness of its streets, and the endless opportunities for discovery around every corner. Whether you're visiting for a weekend getaway or an extended stay, Madrid promises to leave a lasting impression, creating memories that you'll carry long after your journey ends.

As you conclude your adventure through the pages of this guide, remember that Madrid is a city best explored with curiosity and an open heart. There will always be something new to uncover, from the hidden gems of Lavapiés to the quiet cafes tucked away in Chueca. Madrid's magic lies in its ability to surprise, delight, and draw you back, time and again.

So, whether you're planning your first trip or returning for another taste of its vibrant culture, Madrid awaits you with open arms. ¡Hasta pronto, Madrid!

Printed in Great Britain
by Amazon